A Singer's Notebook

A Singer's Notebook

Ian Bostridge

faber and faber

First published in 2011
by Faber and Faber Ltd
Bloomsbury House
74–77 Great Russell Street
London WC1B 3DA

Typeset by Faber and Faber Ltd
Printed in England by CPI Mackays, Chatham

A CIP record for this book
is available from the British Library

ISBN 978–0–571–25245–9

2 4 6 8 10 9 7 5 3 1

To Lucasta, going beyond the Seas

Contents

Foreword

Ian Bostridge came to singing by way of witchcraft. He studied history at Oxford, and even while learning musical repertoire and vocal technique he was also writing *Witchcraft and its Transformations, 1650–1750*. Belief in music's own magical powers has never deserted him; audiences around the world have found something mysterious, other-worldly in his plangent voice. This eerie quality he does not try to explain in *A Singer's Notebook*; instead, he draws on the historian's more mundane desire to set things in context. He wants to place the music he sings, in the history of the art and in society.

All notebooks are collections of bits and pieces of experience, but this one, even in writing done in hotel rooms or on the beach, is carefully shaped. It's not quite fair that a singer should be so gifted a writer. Still, the coherence of this so-called notebook comes also from a persistent set of preoccupations.

One of them is about what's called today 'crossover' in music. Artists in the past didn't worry about it as we now do: in Handel's and Mozart's time, music was thought to have a general appeal; there wasn't separate music for the masses and the elite. Today, the singer seems to cross a chasm between performing Schubert and Cole Porter. Ian Bostridge, who has crossed just that divide, doesn't think it's as great as we may make out, as his reflections on Bob Dylan and Noël Coward show.

The relationship between words and music is the big theme in this notebook, a theme pursued from Monteverdi to Hans Werner Henze, from Benjamin Britten to Mozart. Ian Bostridge is famously a singer who makes words tell; in his performances of Schubert's *Winterreise*, songs that cast a spell of instant intimacy, you can hear and make sense of each twist in Wilhelm Müller's poetry. Essays in the notebook explore what words mean in themselves to the singer, in reflections on writers as diverse as Tolstoy, George Eliot, Schopenhauer and John Updike. For Bostridge – if I can make him the pompous professor he certainly is not – sound and word are aspects of the same meaning; pull them apart, as some singers do in emphasising creamy vowels, and the music is diminished. Perhaps this is the reason that Bostridge so admires Dietrich Fischer-Dieskau, the great baritone whose vocal restraint and clarity projected the sense of what he sang.

Ian Bostridge is, I'd say, a democratic musician. He sings Cole Porter with the same care as he does Handel; he's open to roles some other singers find alien; above all, his goal is to project meaning to the listener rather than invite admiration of his voice. He says little in this notebook about the sometimes ethereal, sometimes abrasive, always expressive qualities of that instrument; perhaps this is a mystery he doesn't want to touch. The context of singing is you, not him.

Richard Sennett

August, 2010

Introduction

But music moves us, and we know not why;
We feel the tears, but cannot trace their source.
Is it the language of some other state,
Born of its memory? For what can wake
The soul's strong instinct of another world,
Like music?
    L.E.L., *Erinna* (1826)

When I first became a full-time singer, back in 1995, I was finishing a long-gestated study of witchcraft theory in the early modern period. Finding the time to dot i's and cross t's in the next couple of years – checking footnotes, refining the argument, preparing an index – didn't seem too irksome or too difficult, and *Witchcraft and its Transformations* was published by Oxford University Press in 1997, by which time I was well into a busy singing career. As a research fellow in history at Oxford I had started writing about music – in which I had next to no formal training – as a form of self-education; but I always intended to join together the two strains of my life in a work that would somehow deal with music in history. It proved more difficult than I had imagined. Finishing a book is rather different from starting one afresh.

Up to that point I'd found very little in the musicological literature that addressed my particular biases as a historian. As far as English-language writers on music went, there seemed to be a yawning divide between abstruse technicalities – either musical or, broadly speaking, post-modernist

– and humanistic engagement with music as a social practice. The sort of cultural history I had studied at university seemed not to have touched most of the writing about music I encountered. What I missed was a nuanced and engaged attempt to relate music to the social and political order that sponsored and consumed it. The writer on music I admired the most was Charles Rosen. His books, lectures and essays stood as a massive and forbidding accumulation of brilliant insight and embodied the broadest of cultural interests; but their technical sophistication, in purely musicological terms (the analysis of theme and key and structure, and the tracing of their relationship to emotional and historical realities) made them inimitable for a novice. Though I understood it but dimly, I still treasure, almost as a talisman, and a reminder of the extraordinary power of music, Rosen's account, in *The Romantic Generation*, of how the postlude of Schumann's *Frauenliebe und -leben* works its magic upon us, playing with time and reminiscence through the use of music's rhetorical device.

Since then, we have had the splendours of Richard Taruskin's six-volume account of the whole of Western music in history for Oxford University Press, at one and the same time a miracle of historical analysis and a statement of profoundly personal taste; Alex Ross's superb one-volume account of twentieth-century music, *The Rest is Noise* – containing, let it be said, not a single piece of off-putting musical notation – my review of which is printed later in this volume; not to mention Tim Blanning's reintegration of music into mainstream political and cultural history, *The Triumph of Music*.

Writing a joined-up book to sit alongside such sophisticated and penetrating studies is a tall order for a jobbing

4

singer. The first piece in this book is the nearest I have got so far to making a bridge between my interests as a historian and my new activity as a musician, trying to uncover a connection between an interest in the grounds of rationality, and a social activity that operates as a sort of embodied escape from the bounds of reason.

Otherwise I have reviewed books and written programme notes, commentaries for my own recordings, pieces for newspapers, and a monthly column for a magazine. These range across most of my activities as a performer, in opera, concert and song. They are often concerned with placing the music within the context of its times – but if my life as a singer, and as a performer in the theatre, has taught me anything intellectually, it is to loosen up on the historical mode of explanation to which I once gave primacy. The continuing vitality of music written in the past lies as much in its connection with timeless human concerns as with the material circumstances of its production. Thinking about both, as well as about the abstract musical construction of a piece, can result in a creative tension that informs and invigorates performance. Performance itself, though, remains a matter of emotional projection and physical engagement. The preparation – be it imaginative, analytical or historical – may be in the broadest sense intellectual, but the power is in the raw connection between audience and performer. Precisely how the voice of the musician and the voice of the composer conspire to move us in concert varies according to composer, performer and type of music; but 'we can cheer ourselves up', as Charles Rosen puts it, 'by reflecting that the greater and the more profound our experience of music becomes, the more we expect the performers to create more than just a pleasing sound, but to move us by illuminating and setting in relief what is most significant in the musical score'.

Ian Bostridge

August 2010

Acknowledgements

The section of this book entitled 'Fugitive Notes' brings together some of the pieces I have written over the years as book reviews, CD notes, programme commentaries and so on. They are reprinted pretty much as they first appeared. Where it seemed necessary or pertinent, I have added a context or further thoughts, which appear in italics. The original articles appeared in a variety of locations: 'Authoritative Voices', 'Handel at the Opera', 'The German Song', 'For the Schubert Bicentenary', 'The Battle of Britten', 'Britten's Letters' and 'Alex Ross: *The Rest is Noise*' were published in the *Times Literary Supplement*; 'French Baroque Music', 'Monteverdi's *Orfeo*', 'My Problem with Mozart', 'Hugo Wolf', 'Janáček', '*The Threepenny Opera*', 'Noël Coward', 'Britten's Song-Cycles for Orchestra', '*Death in Venice*', 'Hans Werner Henze' and '*The Tempest*' appeared in the *Guardian*; earlier versions of '*Billy Budd*' and 'Bob Dylan' appeared in a Barbican programme note and the *Gramophone*; '*Winterreise*' and '*Die schöne Müllerin*' originated as CD liner notes for EMI Classics.

In writing these pieces over the past years, I have accumulated an inexhaustible multitude of debts – practical, intellectual and those of friendship and hospitality. The following deserve particular mention, in no particular order:

Will Eaves at the *TLS*; Charlotte Higgins and Imogen Tilden at the *Guardian*; Professor Gordon Rogoff; Daniel Johnson and Miriam Gross at *Standpoint*; Richard Stokes;

Julius Drake; Professor Richard Sennett; Deborah Warner; Dennis Marks; Seamus Heaney; Professor Alexander Bird; the late Patrick O'Connor; Peter Bloor; Robert Rattray; Annette Allen; Sir Brian McMaster; Sir Keith Thomas; Penelope Gouk; Peter Alward; Bernard Jacobson; David Syrus; Tony Pappano; Graham Johnson; Hans Werner Henze; Thomas Adès; Jeffrey Tate; Leif Ove Andsnes; Dame Mitsuko Uchida; Vikram Seth; Sir Norman Rosenthal; Sarah Christie-Brown; Sophie Daneman; Simon Robson; Ruby Philogene; Richard Jones; Belinda Matthews and Kate Ward at Faber and Faber; Michael Downes; David Miller at Rogers, Coleridge and White; Dietrich Fischer-Dieskau; John Lanchester; Miranda Carter; Theo Zinn; Michael Spencer; Professor John Mullan; Mario Ingrassia; Gerald Moore; Paul Farrington; Daniel Harding; Adam Gopnik; Jean Kalman; Robin Baird-Smith; John Fraser; Ed Gardner; Martin Fitzpatrick; Laurence Cummings; Michael Kersten; Tom Cairns; Emily Campbell; Daisy Cockburn; Emily Best; Professor David Bindman; the late Fausto Moroni; Sally Groves; Rita de Letteriis; Elizabeth Kenny; Jeremy Hall; Jane Haynes; Professor Ralph Wedgwood; Simone Ling; Helen Sprott; the late Harold Pinter; Lady Antonia Fraser; the late Richard Avedon; Professor David Ekserdjian; David Alden; William Lyne; Diana Quick; the Earl and Countess of Harewood; Tabitha Tuckett; Susie Boyt; Rory Stuart; Alex Miller; Sir Alan and Lady Moses; Philip Hensher; Sir Colin Davis; George Nicholson; Morton Lichter; Marshall Izen; Fiona Shaw; Sir Peter Jonas; the late Peter West; the family Baumhauer; Hugo Herbert-Jones; Sita Lieben.

My brother, Mark, first taught me about writing history. My mother Sandy Bostridge's questing musical curiosity has been an example. My children, Oliver and Ottilie, show enormous love and forbearance in the face of my too-frequent absences from home. Their discovery of music is endlessly reinvigorating. My beautiful, brilliant, beloved wife, Lucasta Miller, remains an endless inspiration.

MUSIC AND MAGIC

Given as the Fifth Annual Edinburgh University
Festival Lecture, 2000

My professional career as a singer was, in a very strong sense, necessitated by the Edinburgh International Festival. In the summer of 1994 I was still pursuing that academic career as a research fellow at Corpus Christi College in Oxford, turning my doctoral research on witchcraft into a book. But I was also doing quite a bit of singing and, crucially, I had an agent in London. That year's long vacation I spent in Sydney, Australia, rehearsing, for three weeks, a production of Benjamin Britten's A Midsummer Night's Dream *by the Australian director Baz Luhrmann, a show we then took to the Edinburgh Festival. It was a wonderful immersion in the world of opera, and my first appearance at the Festival. But when I returned to Oxford for the final year of my fellowship, perspectives had shifted on all sides. Public exposure as a performer made my commitment to the academic life seem more than a little compromised. I realised that I could make a career in singing; and my academic supporters (above all, my supervisor and mentor, the great historian Keith Thomas) made it possible for me to make an honourable transition, completing my work and tying up the loose ends.*

For the next twelve or thirteen years, Edinburgh became one of the focuses of my professional life. It only added to the joy of it that my school-friend and best man, the philosopher Alexander Bird, had been appointed to a lectureship at Edinburgh

University which roughly coincided in its duration with my years at the Festival. I gave a song recital every year, and participated in various other, larger projects. So when in 2000 the festival director, Brian McMaster, asked me to deliver the University Festival Lecture, I was not only dazzled, puzzled and honoured (previous lecturers had included giants such as George Steiner, Pierre Boulez and Alfred Brendel): I also saw it as an opportunity to bring together in a single statement, as it were, my historical training and my musical enthusiasm; to explore the connections, to make sense (as we all try to do) of my life.

Many of the preoccupations reflected in the lecture are also to be seen in the subsequent pieces. If I were to sum up what lay behind it all – behind my interests as a historian, and as a singer – it would be a fascination with the limits of rationality, and the possibility (as a rational thinking person, if not always a rational actor in the philosophical sense) of accepting a place in the world for the noumenal or even, loosely speaking, the supernatural. In the seventeenth century systematic thinkers of stature accepted the operation of spirit, of magic, in the world, and saw witchcraft stories as singular proof of that phenomenon. Music's long connection with the traditions of natural magic is part of its historical inheritance, and the central aim of this lecture was to explore that inheritance. That music does have something transcendent about it, that it does allow us to escape the bounds and bonds of rationality – in a measured rather than a crazy way – has always been an instinct in me. At the same time I recognise the difficulty, the impossibility really, of arguing for such a magical capacity. In the end, I have been reminded of Flaubert's passing comment in Chapter 12 of Madame Bovary: *'La parole humaine est comme un chaudron fêlé où nous battons des mélodies à faire danser les ours, quand on voudrait attendrir les étoiles' (Human language is like a cracked kettle on which we beat out tunes for bears to dance to, while all the time we long to move the stars to pity). Music conjures us away from the inadequacies and clumsinesses of ordinary language in trying to express the ineffable. At the same time it remains a human invention, a language, and subject to the constraints of language, however heightened and uncanny it may be. We are still beating on that cracked kettle; and there remains that impassable gulf between the elegant, impassive necessity of the stars, and the intentional, passionate, contingent world of human experience and human culture.*

This lecture has an unusually personal theme for one given in such august and academic surroundings, for which I hope you will forgive me. I've been invited here as a singer; but I once practised as an apprentice historian, the theme of my studies being the disappearance of witchcraft beliefs among educated people during the seventeenth and eighteenth centuries. It's one of life's traditional quests to try to make a meaning out of what may seem random choices; and in my case I can see a very clear, if tendentious link between these two apparently divergent fields, one of them entirely intellectual, in method and subject-matter, the other often almost (as I increasingly discover, and to my dismay) a branch of athletics.

My work on witchcraft forms a small part of a much larger historical endeavour, pursued by a variety of historians, which examines the disappearance of religion as the organising principle of European political, social, cultural and intellectual life over the period 1500–1900. It is, I would suggest, uncontentious to maintain that, in 1500, religion was at the centre of all these pursuits. Political culture, intellectual debate and social customs were so bound up with religion that it is difficult to talk about them as having been autonomous realms of human agency. By 1900, on the other hand, religion had been radically dethroned and replaced in public discourse by, for want of a better word, reason in all its forms. Scientific reason is the paradigm, as represented by (embryonically and at the beginning of the period) the Copernican system; or (in full vigour and towards the end of the period) the formulation of Darwinian natural selection. Economic reason, too, ideological first cousin to Darwinism in its debased form of the survival of the fittest, had triumphed, further consolidating the desacralisation of politics, and of culture more generally.

The question for historians has been whether this process of the triumph of reason has itself been a rational progress. By asking this, I'm not pressing a relativist agenda. The scientific and even economic theories we've ended up with are, quite justifiably, seen as rationally superior to those which we started out with pre-1500. In the roughest possible sense, they work better, and we are well on the way to Francis Bacon's utopian projection of the effecting of all things possible; the question of incommensurability, of whether we can legitimately judge the old by the standards of the new, I leave to the philosophers. But because Reason with a capital 'R' won, doesn't mean that that triumph was inevitable, or outside history. There are all sorts of explanations, many of them social and material, for why reason was adopted in place of faith as governing principle, why the old injunction to believe the impossible, *credo quia absurdum*, itself lost credibility.

This period, roughly 1500 to 1900, saw what Max Weber, one of sociology's founding fathers, called the 'disenchantment of the world', a phrase he adopted from the poet

Schiller. We are caught in what Weber dubbed the iron cage of rationality.

The disappearance of educated witchcraft belief was just a small and precocious part of this process of disenchantment. It involved ditching the idea that the Devil could make pacts with his human agents to effect supernatural ill – in practice, this generally meant routine village malice such as the death of a cow. The change in attribution of such problems coincided with a similar restriction in God's operations in the world, since he was no longer routinely thought to allow the performance of miracles. This evacuation of magic from the everyday world was slow, piecemeal, and by no means uniform. Here is not the place to lay out the details of my argument, but my work on England suggests that it had, in practice, a lot to do with politico-theological debates in the wake of the Glorious Revolution of 1688–9 (in short, the withdrawal of the sacred from the socio-political order), and not much to do (as used to be urged, causally at least) with the 'rise of science'. Some avatars of early modern natural philosophy, indeed, were keen to prove the existence of witchcraft, Robert Boyle of Boyle's Law among them. My work also suggests that all this happened in the course of the early eighteenth century, a little later than the textbooks tell (witchcraft was still a reasonable belief, if not a compulsory one, in 1700; the canonical Irish philosopher Berkeley still urged its appeal in 1712; and it was not finally repealed as a felony until 1736, although by then a dead letter). A comparison with neighbouring, Catholic France suggests a similar story, with a predictably different chronology affected by the vagaries of French politics. Witchcraft was not definitively removed from the French criminal law until the Revolution of 1789. The *Encyclopédie*, the Bible of Enlightenment, included a credulous article on witchcraft in its pages.

My interest in the death of witchcraft – the point at which witchcraft passed into the realm of ridicule for most educated people – is bound up with an interest in the birth of modern rationality, and the attempt to write a history of it that avoids arguments such as 'Well, of course witchcraft belief disappeared, it was nonsense'. That won't wash, because the arguments against witchcraft belief that finally triumphed had been available for at least a century before they did indeed triumph; and what's more, some of the most intelligent thinkers of the seventeenth century did not accept those late sixteenth-century arguments (admirably advanced by the Elizabethan Reginald Scot in his *Discovery of Witchcraft* and repeated almost verbatim nearly a century and a half later by the Hanoverian bishop Francis Hutchinson). We ought to explain the triumph of rationality in a rational manner, but without taking our version of rationality for granted. This involves understanding what was said in the past in favour of supernatural beliefs we now deride; and realising that we have precious few arguments to offer against such beliefs if they are embedded in an entirely alien system of belief and practice. We have to abandon the fantastical brand of intellectual time-travel, in which we return to argue it out with our forebears, when in fact they quite simply wouldn't have seen our point. In a sense it means *reconstructing* the rationality of what are, for us, quintessentially irrational beliefs – beliefs indeed against which we define our own sense of reason – and rendering a certain respect to their proponents.

The connection between all this and music is in the first place highly personal – and perhaps, for somebody with an academic training, disreputable – but if we are living in a disenchanted world, trapped inside rationality's iron cage, it seems to me that music is one of the few areas in which we allow ourselves a socially reputable escape (if an increasingly private one, in this age of alienated technology), an escape that doesn't lose us face with our neighbours, employers or friends. If we have lost our rational licence to believe in witchcraft, in magic, in the possibility of things being effected that are beyond the ken of reason – if supernatural religion has forfeited its legitimacy, or at least its primacy – then music remains one of our few approved routes into exercising a magical sensibility, a sense of the supernatural, the transcendent, the ineffable (using all these words in a fairly loose sense).

This goes beyond, I want to say, a taste for music as narcotic or sublimated physical action. 'The invention of melody', according to the anthropologist Claude Lévi-Strauss, 'is the supreme mystery of man' – and it was one of your previous lecturers, George Steiner, who in his infuriating but courageous study of the relationship between the aesthetic and the realm of the transcendent, *Real Presences*, described the matter of music as 'central to that of the meanings of man, of man's access to or abstention from metaphysical experience'.

In many ways, of course, classical music is rather like a religion. We humble ourselves, performers and audience, before the creative spirit of our ancestors; we perform arcane rituals according to laid-down formulae; we improve ourselves; we imagine ourselves privileged to glimpse something transcendent, some small piece of the infinite. The link to magic is there too, even now. Which modern magus is more like the conjuror of old than the post-Toscanini conductor standing before his (overwhelmingly they're men) orchestra, magic wand in hand, the stance, the rapture very often shamanic in essence. Classical music has its austerities too, of course, and the wriggling discomfort in concerts is reminiscent of nothing if not some church services. But it is also something of a mystery religion, as extraordinary effects and visions are summoned up by techniques that still seem impervious to rational analysis – as will be agreed by anyone who has ever observed the irrational progress of a rehearsal, or been affected to the core by a master composer's use of what ought to be a banal harmony, or baffled by the inadequacy of some piece of arcane high musicological analysis to explain a musical effect.

Whether there is any objective content to the continuing magical/metaphysical impact of music, beyond this social positioning – partly the inheritance of Western classical music's birth in the monastery and the cathedral – is something I want to return to at the more speculative end of this lecture.

The birth of classical music coincided with the high point of magical thinking, and with the birth of classical physics – all part of a renewed energy in European culture, connected, then, superficially, but also at a much deeper level. The sixteenth and seventeenth centuries saw the development of musical styles and techniques, in both performance and composition, which would carry through into the broad tradition of what became classical music. The composers of the early modern period are very clearly our inheritance in a way that Dufay and Ockeghem are not. For E. T. A. Hoffmann it was Palestrina and Beethoven who were the paragons of music as cult. At the same time, this is a period in which the metaphysical aspect of music

was a central part of its identity. This was the case in terms
of traditional cosmology, where the music of the spheres
was a living idea right through to the writings of Johannes
Kepler and beyond; but also at the cutting edge of knowledge, in the area of what is known as natural magic or the
occult philosophy – not magic or occult in the modern sense
of those words, but rather in the sense of hidden operations,
ranging from those we have now absorbed into our mate-
rialist physics, like magnetism, to those we have ultimately
rejected, like the weapon salve (where the weapon which
caused a wound was held to be curative of that wound, and
at a distance). Music obsessed the natural magicians for a
variety of reasons: it dealt in occult influences and healing
powers; it was the prime site for demonstrating the magical
principle of sympathy (resonating strings seemed to demonstrate action at a distance); and it had in Pythagoras a
reputed magus whose discoveries were the foundation of
all subsequent harmonics. Quintessentially musical effects
– consonance and dissonance for instance – were held to be
magical, because they were inexplicable within the traditional categories of Aristotelian, scholastic physics.

At the same time, musical effects were supremely available for experimentation, because the 'scientific' instruments in question – musical instruments, in fact – lay easily
to hand for any self-respecting gentleman amateur. What
is more, the revolution in musical performance which
brought polyphonic consort music and keyboard instruments to the fore necessitated adjustments in tuning and
temperament which, in turn, became part of the research
programme of the new experimental philosophy, which
grew out of, and eventually transformed, the natural magic
tradition.

That supreme icon of the scientific movement, Sir Isaac Newton, is perhaps the best exemplar of this interpretation of music, magic and the new physics. He was barely musical in any normal sense: to quote his biographer, William Stukely, he was 'never at more than one Opera. The first Act, he heard with pleasure, the 2nd stretch'd his patience, at the 3rd he ran away.' None the less, he has been convincingly painted by recent historians as a 'Pythagorean magus', immersed in musical theory as part of his natural magical inheritance. Musical theory was a crucial, if publicly underplayed, component in his understanding of one of the key matters of seventeenth-century natural philosophy, light – through an analogy between the colour spectrum and the musical scale, the seven notes of the scale before returning to the octave considered analogous to the seven colours of the rainbow (red, orange, yellow, green, blue, the strangely superfluous indigo and violet). More significantly, Newton interpreted Pythagoras' views on musical consonance as containing the essence of the inverse square law of gravitation, his dazzling solution to the unity of celestial and terrestrial mechanics and dynamics. He thus reinterpreted the notion of the harmony of the spheres. While Ptolemy had concretised such music, conceiving of crystalline spheres resonating as they rubbed against each other ('There's not the smallest orb that thou beholdst but in his motion like an angel sings,' as Shakespeare famously put it), Newton believed he had recaptured the ancient poetic truth in which the music of the spheres was in fact silent, an abstract harmony, the beautiful proportion of intangible mathematics. 'Apollo's lyre of seven strings', he wrote, 'provides understanding of the motions of all the celestial spheres over which nature has set the sun as moderator.'

Here is a paradox. To assume an identity between conventional symbols and the things that they represent has been seen as a key feature and flaw of magical thinking. Yet Newton's triumph was to equate mathematical functions and physical reality and thus smuggle magic, and a sort of silent music, into the age of reason. Music and mathematics remain, significantly, two areas of modern rational culture in which mystery, ineffability and awe still function. You only have to listen to one of our greatest living mathematicians, Roger Penrose, on either the inspiration of Mozart or the Platonic wonders of mathematical proof, to realise that.

What happened then? To start with, while Newton himself was the 'great amphibium' with a foot in the old world and a foot in the new, the developing classical physics of the next two centuries was increasingly rationalistic and anxious to forgo mystery. Magic was circumscribed, inscribed within Newton's equations, and it ceased to hold much sway elsewhere. The mystical bent and utopian mission of natural magic were tainted after the sectarian excesses of the Civil War and Interregnum in England. And it was England's peerless rationalism that dominated the eighteenth century's intellectual agenda, as Voltaire, for one, was quick to admit. Many topics of natural magical interest, those susceptible of physical experiment – acoustics, in the case of music – became part of the mainstream experimental way. But the notion of any connection between metaphysics or cosmology and the strange, sympathetic, magical power of music was lost.

How, then, might we summarise reason's accommodation with music in this period? Essentially, it was a matter of divorcing the highfalutin theories of music from its practice. The sixteenth century was in this respect a confusing watershed, in which new musical practices were pushing the world of harmony forward, while at the same time depriving it of any cosmological significance. Instrumental sound was no longer available as an embodiment or simulacrum of divine order.

The summation of the old view can be found – prodigiously late and, as it were, stillborn – in the writings, and above all the beautiful illustrations, of the English philosopher Robert Fludd (1574–1637). He shows us God tuning the string of the divine monochord (Pythagoras' old experimental instrument), which stretches from heaven to earth 'embracing all the elements within the unity of its harmonic ratios'. The work of late sixteenth-century musical theorists, such as the great Galileo's father, Vincenzo Galilei, by contrast emphasised the necessary imperfections of contingent sound. Numbers could not sound in themselves; only bodies sounded. And the compromises of temperament necessary to accommodate the discrepancies in the harmonic system meant that audible fact, as one historian has put it, was necessarily divorced from celestial values. 'While sounds may be perfect according to the Pythagorean theory of acoustical laws,' wrote Max Weber in his account of the rational and social foundations of music, 'when sounded together they may produce unpleasant effects.'

It was Weber, returning to where we set out from, who saw the early modern development of music as just one more example of the disenchantment of the world. Not only in the sense that the celestial magic of music was reined in; but also in the sense that the shamanic, cultic expressivity of melody is repressed by the systematic rationality of diatonic harmony, just as most other human activity was submitting to the dictates of arithmetic as apotheosised in the demands of double-entry bookkeeping. For Weber, the history of music to his own time (and he was writing in the early twentieth century, the very moment that the tonal consensus was finally breaking up) was one of creative tension between the magic of melody and the iron cage of harmony, and a melancholy story of human response to melody coarsened and desensitised by the dictates of systems of temperament. 'Temperament', he wrote, 'takes from our ears some of the delicacy which gave the decisive flavour to the melodious refinement of ancient music culture.'

It is fascinating to realise that the patron saint of Western classical music, the two-hundred-and-fiftieth anniversary of whose death we commemorate this year, Johann Sebastian Bach, was still immersed in a version of Renaissance culture, more than a century after it had been discredited. Christoph Wolff's recent and magisterial biography of Bach has as its central conceit the notion of Bach the learned musician, and he quotes C. F. Daniel Schubart – author of the poem 'Die Forelle' (The Trout), which Schubert immortalised in song – to the effect that 'what Newton was as a philosopher, Sebastian Bach was as a musician'. Wolff's interpretation of this sees Bach as a scientist, or rather a natural philosopher in music: an explorer of the musical universe in the spirit of the rational eighteenth century. He was, as another eighteenth-century commentator had it, the 'law maker of genuine harmony', faithful servant of Weber's notion of rationalisation-cum-rationality in music.

This may well be what Schubart had in mind. But I think it makes more sense to see Bach drawing on the old tradition of music as sounding number. Like Newton he was a latter-day Pythagorean, immersed in numerology. Certainly, what little we know of his attitude to music suggests more than the rather austere eighteenth-century theory of affect rooted in an essentially mechanistic view of the body, music as motion inducing emotion in and through the body. Bach's famous annotation to Calov's Bible commentary breathes a headier air: 'N.B. Where there is devotional music, God with his grace is always present.' This suggests a music that could conjure up the divinity in some sense, a belief perilously heterodox if pursued too literally. A recent historian has spoken of Bach, in the metaphysical ambition of his pieces, 'grasping at a cosmic order that was long collapsed by the 1740s'. This, I would suggest, is one reason why the Romantic generation seized upon Bach, retrospectively, as the founder spirit of classical music, music as absolute, music as religion: a cult that dominated the nineteenth century under the banner of Beethoven; which some modernists, Stravinsky for one and perhaps most vigorously, rejected; and which it is still difficult to escape today.

I'll return to that, but for the moment we remain in the eighteenth century with Bach's polar opposite, the adoptive Englishman George Frideric Handel.

Magic disappeared in eighteenth-century England as a reputable area of knowledge; the idea of witchcraft as a crime was discredited by the middle of the second decade. The rationalism that turned away from magic – a proto-Enlightenment, we might call it – had ideological associations in the early eighteenth century with a particular political project: the Whig project, whose ambition was, in essence, to lower the ideological temperature of politics, to discard all those dangerously hot-headed disputes about religion and metaphysics which had so disturbed the fabric of the state from the Civil War of the 1640s through the Glorious Revolution of 1688–9 to the Jacobite uprising of 1715. Witchcraft prosecution had been part of that old world, and one of its last appearances on the public scene was in 1711 (Handel was on his first visit to London that year, settling in 1712), when the conviction for witchcraft of a Hertfordshire woman, Jane Wenham, occasioned a pamphlet war in which high-church extremists supporting conviction were pitted against rollicking free-thinkers who saw the conviction as yet another sore on the body of the Church. The Whig elites who seized control on the Hanoverian accession in 1714, and confirmed their primacy with the failure of the Jacobite rebellion the following year, were at the same time contemptuous of the old magical world-view in which witchcraft was embedded – connected as it was with Stuart divine kingship, the legislation against witchcraft significantly having been enacted under James I in 1604 – and also chary of any such polarising dispute which could stir up ideological passion. They wanted to put a lid on such things, and that was the last to be heard of witchcraft in English public life until the brief flurry surrounding the repeal of both English and Scottish legislation against the crime in 1736.

Handel's life coincides pretty much with the demise of witchcraft. He was born in the year of the last execution in England, 1685. He studied law at the university of Halle, the centre for the last great German debates on the reality of the crime. He arrived in England around the time of the last conviction, as we have seen, and the last major English debates. What is more, Handel being an iconic figure in

Whig culture, the dismissal of witchcraft and magic formed an important, metaphorical undercurrent to his career.

What do I mean by calling Handel an iconic figure of Whig culture? On his death, the composer left money for the erection of a monument in Westminster Abbey, a masterpiece by the French sculptor Louis-François Roubiliac. It's telling that the other great eighteenth-century funerary monument in the Abbey is Rysbrack's Isaac Newton, who, despite his own cryptic mysticism and Unitarian leanings, became the patron saint of rational Whiggery. Earlier in his career, Roubiliac had made another statue of Handel, now in the Victoria and Albert Museum. It shows him as the apotheosis of laid-back Whiggish civility. No wild-eyed creator of transcendent sounds, he is presented instead as an urbane genius, the calm strummer of soothing harmonies, playing on Orpheus' lyre, a cupid at his feet, but in a state of emphatic relaxation. He lounges wigless in cap, loose clothes, and half-relinquished slippers, his elbow resting on a pile of musical scores. The statue, the first such public monument to a British artist, was intended for Vauxhall Pleasure Gardens, which was, to quote the publicity material of the time, 'a Scene . . . of the most rational, elegant, and innocent kind'.

There is a perverse connection with magic here. One of the scores at Handel's elbow is of *Alexander's Feast,* an oratorio that demonstrates the power of music to calm unruly passion, a magical effect whose absence from contemporary music Vincenzo Galilei had been bemoaning more than a century before ('Where are the "miracles" today that are described in the ancient texts?'). Roubiliac's statue is making the same sort of claim for Handel himself. The unruly passions of a pleasure park where men and women of all classes mingled promiscuously could be calmed by his music. Outside the boundaries of Vauxhall, people made the same claim for Handel: political passion and faction could be calmed by his harmony, which he put at the disposal of the Hanoverian succession. Hence Daniel Prat's ode on Handel's organ playing in 1722:

> See! DISCORD of her Rage disarm'd,
> Relenting, calm, and bland as PEACE;
> Ev'n restless noisy FACTION charm'd.

Or Aaron Hill's ode 'on the occasion of Mr Handel's Great Te Deum at the Feast of the Sons of the Clergy' in the 1730s:

> Teach us, undying Charmer, to compose
> Our inbred Storms, and 'scape impending Woes . . .
> And since thy notes can ne'er in vain implore!
> Bid 'em becalm unresting Faction o'er;
> Inspire Content and Peace, in each proud Breast,
> Bid th'unwilling Land be blest.

So, what was left to the magic of music in Handelian England was partly a new mixing together of the metaphor of music as social harmony, and partly a revival of the old task of conjuring the passions, now seen in ultimately mechanistic rather than mystical terms.

Another area of musical magic, metaphorically at least, was virtuosity, an association that lasted into the nineteenth century with the diabolical proficiency of a fiddler such as Paganini. Virtuosity also features in singing; and in Handel's magic operas, as Charles Mackerras has noted, the implausible tessitura of the sorceress is a badge of her magical prowess. In itself, the theatre was seen as magical, dangerously so for some commentators such as Arthur Bedford, clergyman and moral reformer, writing in 1719:

Another Method, made use of at the Play-Houses, is to entertain their Followers with magical Representations, conjuring, or consulting the Devil. This surely can be no great Diversion, at least no proper one for Christians, and may be apt to fill the Heads of raw and ignorant Persons with false and dangerous Notions, as if the Devil's Power and Knowledge was much greater than it is.

'Such Places and Entertainments as these', Bedford concluded, 'must be a disservice to our King, our Church, and our Constitution.'

Yet it is striking how Handel's magic operas actually buttressed the progressive, 'rational' ideology of the regime he served. Handel was, in a commonplace metaphor, viewed as a magician. 'Whilst Mr Handel was playing his part, I could not help thinking him a necromancer in the midst of his own enchantment,' wrote one dazzled contemporary after a rehearsal of *Alcina*. But his 'magic' was at Reason's command.

The magic operas themselves were written in two bursts, three between 1711 and 1715, and two between 1733 and 1735. It is no mere coincidence that these were the two periods in the eighteenth century when public interest in witchcraft in England peaked: the relatively noisy bang of the Wenham trial in 1711; and the whimper of the almost unopposed repeal of the Jacobean witchcraft legislation in 1735–6. The rows over Wenham and over the repeal were both implicated in the construction of a polite and politic consensus over the ejection of the very notion of magic from the body politic – be it the Royal Touch for the King's Evil (scrofula), laws against magic and diabolism, the Divine Right of Kings, or the very religious conception of the state itself. Handel's magic operas, paradoxically full of magical machinery and magical displays of virtuosity, spoke the same language of the triumph of Reason over magic. In that sense they are the Hanoverian, Whig, rational, enlightened counterpart, performed in public, of Inigo Jones's magical and private court masques for the Caroline court a century earlier.

Take *Alcina*, for instance. The evil enchantress of 1735 might represent not so much sorcery, as the enchantment that superstition itself could weave. When at the end of the opera Rogero smashes Alcina's 'infamous urn', a complex metaphor is at work. Alcina's magical realm, conjured from the power of the urn, active force of all the enchantment, disappears. In the world of the opera, the evil sorceress has been overcome; in the world of the composer, the spectacle of opera and the enchantment of music, the suspension of disbelief, has reached its preordained end. In the world of politics, in which eighteenth-century opera undoubtedly played, enlightenment has been achieved. A supernatural nightmare has been banished and human intellect restored.

To underline this ideological strain in the opera, we need only look at the finale. *Alcina* ends, as Handel's operas typically do, with a brief and simple chorus performed by the principals:

> Who has redeem'd us from our senseless State,
> From Night's dark Horrors,
> And brought us back to Life and Liberty . . .
> Who has again reviv'd our Reason and thrown off
> The Veil that cover'd us?
> After the bitter Torments past,
> Our Souls find Peace and smiling Joys at last . . .
> How blest this Day,
> That brings such Ease;
> And now forgetting what we bear,
> Our Hearts know nought but present Peace.

Here, in a libretto book distributed to an audience that would have included the power-brokers and luminaries of Hanoverian society, is the telltale association between the expulsion of magic, the triumph of rationality, and the achievement of (social) peace. The keywords are those of Whig ideology: under the current dispensation reason is revived, the horrors of dark night are forgotten, liberty has been restored, and nothing but peace is known, peace and ease. This was the complacent Whig view of the Hanoverian dispensation, and Handel sang its song.

We've seen music and magic inextricably bound together in the Renaissance; and we've seen music symbolically exorcising magic from the body politic in the pre-Enlightenment. It was the philosophers of the Romantic period who raised the stakes again; but they did so in a context in which their metaphysics was utterly divorced from scientific endeavour, in a way that the Renaissance natural magicians had not known. The really interesting matter of music – what I have called the 'magic' of music, and what Renaissance theoreticians might have studied under the rubric of sympathy, binding together emotional affect, sympathetic vibration and the structure of the universe (a world-view no longer available to us) – has been essentially abandoned by modern science to become a backwater. Why does music mean so much to us? Scientific accounts of music – I recall a recent summary in *The Economist* – remain thin and unconvincing, an unnourishing brew of superficiality and question-begging evolutionary psychology (at least Steven Pinker's characterisation of music as 'aural cheesecake' recognises the inability of evolutionary science to grapple with it); philosophical accounts (I think of Roger Scruton's marvellous writing on music) are intriguing but essentially speculative or largely poetic in their appeal, cut off from the sharp end of scientific reckoning.

It was the Romantic philosophers writing at the beginning of the nineteenth century who raised music once again to the pinnacle, certainly as the aesthetic paradigm of absolute art, and in some cases as the centre of a new metaphysic or the ground bass of a new religion. In one sense this was just the wheel, as ever, turning: Romanticism as a rebellion against what seemed the rational calculation of the Age of Enlightenment. It was also reinforced by, perhaps even invented in response to, the new music dominated by the ambition and creative energy of Beethoven. If there was a cult of music in the nineteenth century, against which the modernists rebelled, Beethoven stood at its head. The eighteenth century's supposed lack of creative ambition – Haydn's *Creation* was much mocked for its capitulation to the aesthetic of illustrative imitation – was spurned by a nineteenth century in thrall to a notion of absolute music that could match the ineffability of the Hegelian absolute. E. T. A. Hoffmann, phantasmagoric fabulist and Beethovenian devotee, summed it up when he declared that instrumental music, freed as it was from text, was 'the most Romantic of all the arts', awakening 'an infinite yearning towards an unknown realm'. It was the very lack of signification in music, its emptiness if you like, that allowed it somehow to gesture towards the unknowable absolute which was at the centre of the dominant idealist philosophy. For some Romantic thinkers, music, as a result, became a sort of religion: 'the ultimate mystery of faith, the mystique, the completely revealed religion', as the poet Ludwig Tieck affirmed.

Schopenhauer is without doubt the best-known exemplar of the Romantic exultation in (if Schopenhauer ever did anything as cheery as exult) and exaltation of music. For this philosopher, music 'exhibits itself as the metaphysical to everything physical in the world . . . We might, therefore, just as well call the world embodied music as embodied will.' I cannot enter here into the complexities of Schopenhauer's conception of will, and of the homology between the processes of music and the activity of the will. I want to give just a flavour of his endeavour by quoting his account of melody:

As rapid transition from wish to satisfaction and from this to a new wish are happiness and well-being, so rapid melodies without great deviations are cheerful. Slow melodies that strike painful discords and wind back to the keynote only through many bars, are sad, on the analogy of delayed and hard-won satisfaction . . . The short, intelligible phrases of rapid dance music seem to speak only of ordinary happiness which is easy of attainment. On the other hand, the *allegro maestoso* in great phrases, long passages, and wide deviations expresses a greater, nobler effort towards a distant goal, and its final attainment. The *adagio* speaks of the suffering of a great and noble endeavour that disdains all trifling happiness.

This is both ambitious for music, while at the same time being somewhat inadequate to it. It is, necessarily but with a diminishing return for Schopenhauer's argument, tied to the music of his own time – slow melodies, fast melodies, the *allegro maestoso*, *adagio* and, above all, the diatonic system itself, with its sense of home key and alienation from that place of repose. But, at the same time, it is inadequate to much of the great music of its era; one can imagine Schubert constructing 'short, intelligible phrases of dance music' which could speak of far more than the 'ordinary happiness which is easy of attainment'.

Of course, this is largely a matter of the inadequacy of language to music, something of which Schopenhauer himself makes much. Language can capture, somehow, the magic of music. Proust is the paramount example in literature, and music is one of the great themes of *A la recherche du temps perdu*. For instance, see his exquisite description (in passing) of the relationship between music and words in a vocal piece, the music compared to laughter 'tracing an invisible surface on another plane'. But it's only when language, as poetry or metaphor, partakes of the nature of music, that it can capture its essence – however fleetingly, as Proust himself recognised. Music's way of 'codifying' human experience cannot be 'resolved into rational discourse'. That's the point. Yet at the same time Proust was fully aware of the claims of music. Here is his narrator, talking about the fictional composer Vinteuil:

Vinteuil's last compositions were ultimately declared to be his most profound. And yet no programme, no subject matter supplied any intellectual basis for judgement. One simply sensed that it was a question of the transposition of profundity into terms of sound.

We're back to the Romantic world-view here, easy to ridicule – perhaps the 'transposition of profundity into terms of sound' is even meant to be a little absurd, though Proust was deeply influenced by Schopenhauer – but it is a vision of music that still appeals, especially in the reception of the classics. They are more than mere entertainment, surely: they somehow carry importance with them, they seem to say more than they possibly ought to be able to say, they connect with an elsewhere (another country as Proust puts it), they remain magical in the sense of carrying effect beyond all analysable cause. I come back to that word 'ineffable'. But there's precious little justification for such a stance in the disenchanted world in which we live. It's a standing affront to the reductionism of the age.

The cynical, no doubt sensible, and certainly appealing response of the trained historian is to see fetishisation and reification simultaneously at work. Trained up in the Western system from our earliest years, we view so-called classical music (of which, musically speaking, the pop musics of our times tend to be superficially radical but fundamentally conservative re-enactments), as 'natural' in some sense. Music, a thoroughly cultural phenomenon, is experienced as though it were part of the natural world (rather like money, in fact); a given, rather than something endlessly reconstructed and renegotiated in social space. That's why music can function so well as what the musicologist Nicholas Cook calls a 'hidden persuader', one of the key tricks of the advertiser, playing upon us unawares, lending authenticity to an otherwise all-too-transparent sales pitch. Music, as he puts it, effaces its own agency. With more aesthetic purpose, the soundtrack of a film can very often secretly create that sense of coherence, conviction and significance; you can even catch yourself doing it with your own quotidian existence when you drive along playing music in the car.

But the fact that historically and socially music is learnt behaviour, varying by culture, doesn't stop me thinking that there's something magical in its very ability secretly to persuade or lend significance. For all I know, other musics may do the same (many of them certainly have similar roots in religious ritual, and music of some sort seems to be a universal feature of human life); and I may be buried so deep inside Western music's conjuring trick that I can't see my way out to a clear view. But – to abandon relativism for a moment – there is no reason to reject out of hand the notion that Western classical music as it has developed over the past five hundred years is, to use an odd descriptive term, a 'technology' particularly suited (like many other quintessentially 'Western' technologies) to performing a task that may be of universal human significance.

What is that task though? I've talked about magic, about profundity, about ineffability and effects beyond causes. Well, I return to Romanticism, in a late form: the Romanticism of Ludwig Wittgenstein, another Schopenhauer aficionado. He was a key figure in the 'linguistic' revolution in twentieth-century philosophy – which reconstructed many of the old metaphysical problems in terms of the philosophy of language rather than of 'the world out there' – and also a great lover of music. One of his most gnomic, and famous, utterances cries out to be inserted in this debate. It's much more beautiful in German, so I'll give you the original first:

> Wovon man nicht sprechen kann, darüber muß man schweigen.

Or, 'What we cannot speak about, we must pass over in silence.' Silent in words, beyond reasoning, yes – but silent altogether, not necessarily.

Classical music is one of the few ways out of this impasse, and Western music, since it was cast out of the rational natural philosophical pantheon in the seventeenth century, and at the same time began to codify its own rational structure, has become one of the ways of talking about all the things we cannot rationally talk about – the nature of existence, the quality of time, non-existence, annihilation, cosmic regret. And on that rather portentous note, I had better stop.

STANDPOINT

I started writing a column for the new monthly magazine Standpoint *in 2008, really as a sort of discipline. Over the past fifteen or so years as a singer, I have tried on several occasions to write a diary, but have never managed for more than a week or so. When I recorded one on old-fashioned cassette tapes, often in the bath at the end of the day, during the whole five-week rehearsal period for Deborah Warner's staging of Seamus Heaney's new translation of Janáček's* The Diary of One Who Vanished, *inspired mainly by the wittily recursive possibilities of writing a diary about* The Diary, *I didn't get very far – not surprisingly. I had, I now realise (listening back to the tapes) very little to say. Or rather, I didn't have the energy, in the midst of struggling with the production, to struggle to say what needed to be said. One of the most extraordinary things about great subjective writing – Proust, say, laying out, anatomising and characterising a train of thought – and also about great diary writing, is the capacity to be dogged, not to let go until every little strange and unexpected turn of thinking has been teased out. Much of what I have listened to of these tapes, ten years later, seems to veer away from what was actually interesting about the work, or to obsess with practical or factual trivia – times of meetings, names of participants, meals eaten, objective tasks undertaken. Performing work is fascinating and creatively engaging, both in the encounter with canonical musical and literary texts, and in the opportunities it offers for collaboration with imaginatively gifted people – writers, directors, musicians, actors – but I have never been able to capture this in the essentially subjective,*

41

stream-of-consciousness, informal form of the diary.

So these pieces for Standpoint *are partly in lieu of a diary: another attempt, since I was given the wonderful freedom to write about whatever I happened to be doing or thinking about that month. Some of them reflect the old obsessions about the magic of music, some ruminate on the actual business of singing and performing. The other discipline – apart from that of the monthly deadline – was to try to find a different way of writing, to loosen up a little after all my years of academic work and the scrupulous avoidance, drummed into the academic brain, of the first-person singular. Really a discipline towards indiscipline, an attempt to find a more relaxed form of expression. Maybe gearing up to write a diary, who knows? Anyway, after a year of writing, I took a rather grandly named 'sabbatical' from* Standpoint *to prepare this collection of fugitive pieces. Where I've had some further thoughts on the subjects discussed, I've added them.*

June 2008

Bach is the irreducible indispensable of classical music. You would be hard pressed to find a performer who would admit to disliking him; and composers don't use him – as Benjamin Britten used Beethoven and Brahms and Strauss, for example – to define a contrary aesthetic agenda. He is, as much as a dead white male can be, universal; and also, in a sense, pure. Concert pianists who spend a lot of their time with the Romantic longing that dominates the piano repertoire, from late Mozart to Rachmaninov, have been known to cleanse themselves with an icy immersion in the Bach keyboard works first thing in the morning.

In Bach there seems something morally uplifting: he was a supremely gifted artist, never to be surpassed, who founded an unbroken tradition in musical art, yet who was unwittingly, as it were, leading a day-to-day existence of surpassing ordinariness and, yes, decency. An assiduous, if prickly, municipal servant in Leipzig, he was a devoted father, married twice, to women who bore him twenty children between them: one in the eye for the supposed artistic imperative to excess and irresponsibility of a Lord Byron or a Jimi Hendrix.

Bach means 'stream' in German – in his own era and area of Germany there were so many of the Bach family in music that it had also come to mean 'musician' – and Bach's purity, like that of limpid water, makes for an easy contrast with the worldly, commercially minded, theatrical Handel, whose name is reminiscent of German words for shop and business.

There is something to this notion. There is more in Handel of an Italian *sprezzatura*, music for pleasure; while Bach speaks more to the German taste for the earnest and the metaphysical. Handel died rich; Bach comfortable. Handel was one of music's great plagiarists, repeating himself and stealing from others with gay abandon, while Bach seems to have generated most of his musical material himself. On the other hand, George Frideric Handel was a deeply religious man; and Johann Sebastian Bach was certainly not an angelic musical aesthete. None the less, the latter has achieved a sort of pre-eminence in music, a saintly quality, which has made his reputation immune to the vagaries of fashion or style, ever since the rediscovery of his music by the Romantic composers more than a century and a half ago.

After a long break – six years or so – I have been spending a lot of time with Bach over the past weeks on two very contrasting projects: a *St John* and a *St Matthew Passion*. St John's Gospel is, of the four, the most theologically minded and mystical. Nevertheless, Bach makes of it, in his *St John Passion*, a work more deeply personal and thrustingly dramatic than the monumental and later *St Matthew Passion*, a work that he consciously saw as part of his legacy.

In the *St John Passion*, singing, as I do, the part of the Evangelist, the storyteller, it is very easy and, I think, proper to become involved in the act of narration and in the emotions of the narrative (though some people, misunderstanding the whole thrust of eighteenth-century German piety, find it vulgar). Bach takes very seriously the notion that St John was a witness to these events, a friend and disciple of Jesus Christ and the comforter of his mother. While the *St Matthew Passion*'s narrative is just as dramatic, with as much tenderness, violence and passion, the greater number of reflective arias, sung as if by present-day Christians who meditate on and participate in the drama, both interrupt the narrative more and lend the whole work a more universal aspect.

One particular moment in the *Matthew* struck me, for the first time, as a manifestation of the mundanity (in the best sense) of Bach's genius. The aria for alto and oboes da caccia with choir, 'Sehet', speaks of Christ stretching out his arms to gather in the oppressed sinners, the 'verlassnen Küchlein' or abandoned chicks. What makes that homely image of Christ as a sort of mother hen so tender and moving is the extraordinary sound that the oboes make together: a clucking, farmyard noise.

My *St John Passion* took place in London, with the brilliant choral director and conductor Stephen Layton, and a band of old instruments – dramatic, almost theatrical, but deeply felt. Mannerism is often used as a negative term in criticising classical singing or playing, but in fact mannerism and its inflections are at the heart of what we do. What we have regained by using old instruments is a whole series of eighteenth-century mannerisms that had been lost; ways of articulating and phrasing which modern instruments and styles of singing, with their emphasis on line, blend and consistency of palette, had almost obliterated.

Singing the *Matthew* with the Boston Symphony Orchestra and the legendary Bernard Haitink should, I suppose, have been very different. It was, amazingly, Haitink's first performance of a Bach Passion. In all his years at the Concertgebouw Orchestra in Amsterdam – which has a long and distinguished Bach tradition – he was never asked to conduct a Bach Passion, to his regret.

A modern orchestra like the Boston brings something different to these pieces, of course. Despite the virtues of all that has been discovered and revived by the period-practice specialists, it would be a perverse, self-denying ordinance that banned modern orchestras from playing this music. These are wonderful musicians whose musicality has been formed in the shadow of Bach. He is a deep composer, literally – one whose works function on many different levels; there are aspects of the music that only modern instruments can illuminate. There is no right and wrong. And in this case we were under the benign supervision of a great conductor, one who knows when to intervene and when to stand back and let it happen. It was a great way to come back to the *Matthew*.

But if I ask myself why I have missed these pieces so much, why they were for ten years such an important part of my singing year, I have to say that, typical Anglican agnostic that I am, they satisfied my religious instincts. I don't think that's just woolliness on my part. Bach's music represents something very special: an end and a beginning.

He is a late exemplar of the Renaissance sensibility that saw music as an embodiment and expression of the Divine order; composers who wrote after him, even composers who were truly religious or who were profoundly influenced by him, wrote music that lacked the confident expressivity of that metaphysical-cum-religious framework.

Immersing ourselves in his music, which harnessed supreme technical skill to a coherent vision of a God-infused world, allows us an inner vision (an aural one) of that long-lost sense of order and belonging.

There is, of course, a tension at work here, between the high-minded view of Bach as a window onto the spiritual, as a universal spirit, essentially a Romantic view; and a just reluctance to eschew the full-blooded humanity and theatricality that Bach's Passions can offer. On the one hand the metaphysical, intellectual flights of a fugue in full flow; on the other, Bach's response both to detail of narrative (Peter warming himself in the courtyard of the high priest, the observation that it was early in the morning) and to the human predicament of Christ, his followers, even Pontius Pilate. The theatrical possibilities of Pilate's remark to Christ, 'Was ist Wahrheit?' (What is truth?), remain fascinatingly open. Is it a joke or a historical/philosophical profundity? As Ann Wroe points out in her marvellous Pilate: The Biography of an Invented Man, *'it is an odd moment, marked in John's original Greek by an abrupt ending to the paragraph; the words are literally left dangling': something one might try to reflect as a Bach Evangelist by leaving a slightly overlong pause, a caesura which musically breaks the metrical flow. It is certainly an example of how dramatic detail can be informed by the metaphysical.*

The paradox is that it has been the authenticists, the commissariat of early music, the anti-Romantics, who have shown a bias (thankfully now in retreat) towards emotional detachment in this music. But we can have our cake and eat it here, surely, for the subjectivism and visceral emotion of early eighteenth-century German religion, forged in the aftermath of the huge destruction and slaughter of the Thirty Years War (so different from the aesthetic detachment and fear of sentimentality that followed the Great War), is as much a part of Bach as his cosmic striving. Another feature that distinguishes Bach from his compatriot Handel, a naturalised Englishman who adopted the Anglican, middle way. Mein Herz schwimmt im Blut *is, and has to be, a cantata by Bach, not Handel.*

In this piece I called Bach irreducible and indispensable and, of course, as I sat down to write this coda news reached me of the distinguished pianist Stephen Hough's apostasy (as revealed in a blog on the Telegraph *website) – the inevitable exception that proves the rule:*

I recognise with crystal-clear clarity that Bach is a greater composer than Mompou, in the way that Rembrandt is a better painter than Rockwell. To put the two composers on the same level would be risible, and the Spaniard would be the first to be nonplussed with embarrassed laughter. Yet, I don't get Bach, even whilst I understand his towering genius . . . but I do get Mompou.

And I forgot another, historical, exception: Wagner's hideous diatribe 'Das Judenthum in Musik' in which Bach's (heartless?) formality, so appealing to the despised Mendelssohn, is opposed to the 'purely human expression' of Beethoven.

July 2008

Singers spend an inordinate amount of time travelling and staying in hotels. While rock stars are reputed – and maybe contractually required – to trash their luxury suites, whiling away the nights, and probably days, between gigs in an orgy of drink, drugs and, well, orgy, classical singers in their more modest accommodation pursue a quieter life in which rest plays an enormous role.

The physical requirements of the unamplified voice are neurosis-inducing, and the question of how to fill the downtime is perennial. I've always read a lot, but sometimes reading is just that little bit too strenuous. I used to watch CNN a lot, but the endless repetition of the increasingly extruded and etiolated news cycle was, in the end, too much. For me, as for many other travellers, the DVD has been a godsend, and the HBO series *The Sopranos* hit the spot. If I wasn't OD-ing on drugs, drink and dissolution, at least I could quietly watch some other people doing it.

When, as a distant echo from the depths of popular culture, I first became aware of *The Sopranos*, I did, of course, pathetically assume that it was about singers. It would be nice to pretend that *The Sopranos* was a television series about a hard-bitten gang of coloraturas and lirico spintos, who indulge themselves in a spot of casual violence, racketeering and lap-dancing.

It was only when I read a long and appreciative essay review in the *New York Review of Books*, a year or two back, that I realised that here was something not to be missed, and that the subject-matter was the New Jersey Mob.

So for the past four months, while travelling the world singing Bach, Schubert, Britten, Kurt Weill and Mozart, I have had a disorientating and intermittent immersion in more than a hundred hours of the Soprano family, their joys (not so many) and woes: Tony, the boss's murderous mother, Livia (surely named after the Emperor Augustus' poisoner of a wife); Tony's sessions with his psychotherapist, Dr Jennifer Melfi; his troubles with the New York family across the bridge from New Jersey; the killings he commissions; the punches he throws; the school and college trajectories of his children, Anthony Junior (dropout) and Meadow (high-achieving Columbia undergrad).

One of my teachers, the great Swiss tenor Hugues Cuenod, who sang Noël Coward's *Bitter Sweet* in New York in the 1920s, Monteverdi madrigals with Nadia Boulanger in the 1930s, created the auctioneer in Stravinsky's *The Rake's Progress*, made his Met debut in his ninth decade, and has just turned 106, told me that the paintings I saw, the books I read and, by implication, the films I watched should all feed my imagination as a singer.

All these forms of relaxation are also meritorious labour, which seemed a nice way to make a living. *The Sopranos* makes an obvious contribution to my singing of Weill's gangster ballad, 'Mack the Knife', I suppose. But the theme that has resonated most through my work in the past months has been that of children, parenthood and sacrifice, in the context of concert performances of Mozart's first great opera, *Idomeneo*.

The plot of *Idomeneo* is simple: Idomeneo saves himself from a storm by promising the life of the first living creature he sees in sacrifice to Neptune. That creature is his own son, Idamante, who is saved only by the love and self-sacrifice of the Trojan (and hence enemy) princess, the captive Ilia. Idomeneo abdicates; Idamante and Ilia will rule in his stead. Only Electra, Idamante's original intended, and Agamemnon's daughter, is left raging and unreconciled, with music of extraordinary ferocity.

If, as so many commentators have observed, *The Sopranos* is not really about the Mob, but about the

American family and its discontents, neither is *Idomeneo* really about the relationship between the mythic and human orders in an archaic Greek kingdom. The trend in musicological writing about *Idomeneo* – and, it should be said, in many of the reviews of our performances of the piece – has been to emphasise the formal aspects of the opera, its heroic cast, its grandeur. This seems to me almost entirely a mistake.

Like *The Sopranos* – which starts with an uncle and mother trying to murder the central character, and ends with that same character murdering a nephew who has been a son to him – *Idomeneo* is obsessed with the wrongs, the losses, the status of children and adopted children.

How can we do our best for them, how protect them, how save them? These questions run through the opera with an extraordinary urgency from the outset: Ilia lamenting the loss of her father and brothers in the Trojan Wars; Idamante desperately receiving the (false) news of his father's death; the profoundly moving recognition scene, in which father and son recognise each other after a ten-year separation, and the father, burdened by his terrible oath, refuses to acknowledge him; the funereal *largo* as Idamante enters to be sacrificed by his father, clad in white, his words – 'Padre, mio caro padre, ah dolce nome' – set to music of melting tenderness.

Even Electra, so often seen as peripheral, if musically magnificent, has a parallel history, which is the reason for her asylum in Crete: a history barely mentioned in the opera, but looming over it. Electra has a whole series of skeletons in the cupboard: her sister Iphigenia sacrificed by her father, her father murdered by her mother and her mother's lover, she herself complicit in the murder of her mother. The same theme is reiterated again and again in music of fury, emptiness, pathos and desperation.

Mozart's own relationship with his father was very much in his mind in the years leading up to the composition of *Idomeneo*. It was while he was in Paris in 1778, researching librettos for a new opera, that his mother died. Mozart was, for the first time, a lone adult, responsible for himself. The relationship with his father, in Salzburg, entered a crucial phase, resulting in a semi-estrangement. The dynamics of self-sacrifice – the son for the father, the father for the son – which were part of a child prodigy's existence (and Mozart had been the great child prodigy of the age), may not have been at the front of Mozart's mind, and may not account for the selection of such a personally appropriate libretto. The choice was that of the court at Munich, although the musicologist Daniel Heartz has argued that Mozart may have found the 1712 Danchet original in Paris. Regardless of this, however, it cannot but be the case that these family concerns inform and infuse the emotional aesthetic of this very great opera.

In the summer of 1783, during a visit by Wolfgang and his wife Constanze to Salzburg, the Mozart family sang through the great quartet from the third act of *Idomeneo*, in which Idamante resolves to leave his father, 'Andro ramingo e solo'. Mozart would have sung Idamante; his wife Ilia; his sister Nannerl, Electra; his father Leopold, Idomeneo. Mozart ran out of the room in tears.

Idomeneo was the first operatic role I performed as an adult: for one night only, in the 'B' cast of the Oxford University Operatic Society production in the Oxford Playhouse, circa 1990. I was comically inexperienced to be playing such a role on stage, and I still remember the whole of one side of my body going numb as I made my entrance, shipwrecked but clearly overexcited, and suffering from a severe case of adrenalin poisoning. Whether I was too young (twenty-five or so), either in terms of vocal colour or of physical plausibility, is a moot point. Mozart's first Idomeneo, for the Munich premiere, was Anton Raaf, aged sixty-six; his second, Giuseppe Antonio Bridi, in the concert performance of the revised version at the Auersperg Palace in Vienna, was just twenty-three. Singing the role as a professional nearly twenty years later, I think I could reasonably feel I'd achieved a happy mean.

The issue of heroism is a more interesting one. Heroism is one of the great, unexpected, controversies in opera. Living, as we do, in an anti-heroic age, much of the thrust of modern productions of 'heroic' operas – especially Wagner – is to deconstruct the whole notion of heroism. Many in the critical community – the Wagnerians especially – find this an evasion. As Roger Scruton eloquently puts it in his book Understanding Music:

Wagner's mature operas concern heroes who move in a mythic realm, and who are prompted by emotions which have been lifted free of ordinary human contingencies and endowed with a cosmic significance and force . . . To take these operas seriously is to be drawn into a peculiar modern project, which is that of remaking the gods out of human material. This project . . . identifies both the artistic triumph of Wagner, and the hostility with which that triumph is so often greeted.

If it doesn't seem too much of a cop-out or a sedative to properly enlivening controversy, surely we can accommodate both approaches? And others too. Certainly, speaking as a resolutely non-heroic (or even anti-heroic) singer – by vocal necessity as much as by choice or disposition – a family-therapy approach to Idomeneo *appeals as much as did Chéreau's Marxist-cum-*

Freudian take on Wagner's Ring *at Bayreuth in the 1970s.
Hugues Cuénod sadly died in 2010, aged 108.*

August 2008

Music performed at home was one of the defining experiences of the nineteenth-century bourgeoisie. It inspired
some of the greatest masterpieces of what has become the
concert repertoire – especially songs and solo piano pieces –
as well as a lot of underrated music that is less often heard
publicly, precisely because it was designed to be performed
by friends, such as vocal ensembles with piano, and pieces
for four hands. Thanks to the gramophone and its successor technologies, the tradition of performing at home has
largely died out. Every so often, though, friends ask musicians to play at home, or musicians want to try out a new
programme in a friendly environment, and *Hausmusik*, as
the Germans call it, is resurrected.

Of course, performing tricky or emotionally exposing
music to an audience of friends or acquaintances a couple
of feet from you – literally within spitting distance, if you're
a singer – in somebody's drawing room, is often far more
intimidating than standing on the stage of the Teatro alla
Scala or Carnegie Hall. And being in the audience can also
be challenging. A couple of weeks ago, a friend asked about
twenty of us to come to a party with music, only announc-
ing once we'd all arrived that we would be hearing Zemlinsky's piano transcription of Mahler's Sixth Symphony as
the centrepiece of the evening's entertainment. Even the
most committed Mahlerians among us found the prospect
of an hour and twenty minutes of piano transcription for
four hands in a smallish room daunting. As it turned out,

it was one of the most memorable musical experiences of my life – transparent and compelling, lacking the rhetorical, clever orchestration that, as with Mahler's songs, often overwhelms the directness and authenticity of the musical material.

The Mahler was followed by something utterly different. Marina Poplavskaya, the Russian soprano who has just been playing Elisabetta in Verdi's *Don Carlo* at Covent Garden, sang an unaccompanied Russian folk-song, something about love and magic, melancholy, heartbreak – I can't remember exactly. It doesn't matter, though at the time the words (which I couldn't follow) were a crucial part of the experience, of its emotional contours and emotional impact. It was timeless and itself magical. It embodied something that is at the same time the touchstone of great performance and almost impossible to capture in words: authenticity.

In *War and Peace*, Tolstoy arranges for young, impressionable Natasha Rostova to have two musical experiences, placed very close together in the architecture of the novel, clearly meant to shed light on each other and speak together to the reader. In Book VII, in one of those set-pieces that ties the book to the Homeric epic tradition, the Rostovs go on a wolf-hunt. Six chapters of hunting are followed by a night in a simple Russian home. The host plays and sings:

. . . as peasants sing, with full and naive conviction that the whole meaning of a song lies in the words, and that the tune comes of itself, and that apart from the words there is no tune, which exists only to give measure to the words. As a result of this the unconsidered tune, like the song of a bird, was extraordinarily good. Natasha was in ecstasies.

Book VIII shows us, by contrast, a night at the opera, which 'after her life in the country, and in her present serious mood seemed grotesque and amazing to Natasha'. Everything is artificial and external, alienated, so 'pretentiously false and unnatural that Natasha at first felt ashamed for the actors and then amused at them'. When she eventually falls under the spell of the bizarrerie on stage, which now seems, in Tolstoy's words, 'quite natural', it is because she has submitted to the world she has found herself in, given up on the authentic life of Book VII. The next step in her corruption is her planned elopement with the scapegrace Kuragin, who had flirted with her at the opera.

While I'm not so sure about the terrible moral effects of going to the opera, Tolstoy does highlight one of the dilemmas faced by the performing artist: the tensions and contradictions implicit in the relationship between art and artifice.

One of the worst criticisms, supposedly, that can be made of a performer is that he or she is 'mannered'. It seems to me that, in fact, this is an accusation without any traction at all; we may not like the particular way in which a performance is mannered, but all artistic performance is artificial, contrived, mannered. Tolstoy's unmediated art, as natural as birdsong, is a useful myth, a shimmering ideal, a fictional but intangible goal. When we perceive authenticity in performance, it is most often because the artist as artificer has been at work – coaxing, striving, editing, experimenting, failing – to produce something that, in its harnessing of technical accomplishment and mannerism appears assured and expressive. It was surely Marina Poplavskaya's craft as a singer that allowed her to achieve such authenticity of expression that night.

For those working a lot with Lieder – the songs of Schubert, Schumann, Wolf, Brahms, their contemporaries and followers – this issue of authenticity is particularly moot. The artifice of opera, which Tolstoy so hated, is more or less accepted by its audiences as a necessary feature of the art-form, to be enjoyed and, occasionally, wonderfully, transcended. Recitals of Lieder are much more naked: not just the lack of costume, set or make-up, but the dramatic conceit of a direct communication between one human being and another (you can usually see your audience) in music that does not, as far as the singer is concerned, make an issue of display or technique, though much vocal technique may actually be deployed.

It is crucial that while the outcome may seem spontaneous – and is indeed spontaneous, in that it isn't choreographed in the way an opera is – it does nonetheless depend on artifice and on craft: not only the singerly craft of supporting the voice, managing its registers and so on, but the specifically Lieder-singing craft so perfectly expressed by Tolstoy – working with a pianist to make sure that 'the tune comes of itself . . . that apart from the words there is no tune, which exists only to give measure to the words'.

This doesn't mean that the words are more important, or that the pianist doesn't exist, but that the pianist and singer work together, in immense detail, with alertness to rhythmic fluctuation and harmonic accentuation, to produce a seamless whole and the illusion of true expression – which is, somehow, true.

Tolstoy was an amateur composer, a fine pianist apparently, who declared music to be 'the shorthand of emotion'. At the same time, an ambivalence towards music, as towards sex (which he also enjoyed well into his dotage, despite his commitment to a celibate ideal), runs through much of the work of his maturity. The operatic decadence that envelops Natasha in War and Peace *prior to her elopement has become a mere satirical squib in the opening of* Anna Karenina. *The engagingly louche Stiva Oblonsky dreams of a dinner 'served on glass tables – yes, and the tables sang "Il mio tesoro" . . . no, not exactly "Il mio tesoro", but something better than that; and then there were some kind of little decanters that were really women'. In the novel as a whole, as the critic Edward Wasiolek puts it, 'Tolstoy sees sex as a massive intrusion on a person's being and a ruthless obliteration of the sanctity of personhood.' It's difficult to think of a more sparkling image of the obliteration of personhood than women becoming decanters.*

The connection between sex and music is finally made utterly, radically and psychotically explicit in the late story, The Kreutzer Sonata, *inspired by Beethoven's sonata for violin and piano – the story in turn inspired Janáček's string quartet of the same name. Pozdnyshev, a stranger on a train, tells his fellow passengers the story of how he came to kill his wife, of whose murder he has just been acquitted. A performance of the 'Kreutzer' Sonata at their house, she accompanying a violinist 'half professional, half man of the world', had inspired in Pozdnyshev a frenzy of jealousy which ended in his stabbing her to death. Much of the story can be understood as an aesthetic reworking of Tolstoy's sexual ideals, which he represents through the medium of a madman – a brilliant example, as Chekhov recognised, of the artist trumping the ideologue. But Pozdnyshev himself is insistent that the problem was the music: 'He and his music were the real cause of it all. At my trial the whole thing was made to look as though it had been caused by jealousy. Nothing could have been further from the truth.'*

Through Pozdnyshev, Tolstoy presents a vision of music as powerful, overwhelming, almost sacred. The first, presto movement (which, interpreted sexually, suggests a level of violence and frustration matched only by the piano interlude in Janáček's Diary of One Who Vanished) is 'a fearful thing'. 'Such pieces', Pozdnyshev declares, 'should be played only on certain special, solemn, significant occasions when certain solemn actions have to be performed, actions that correspond to the nature of the music.' For the protagonist of The Kreutzer Sonata, *music divorced from its social function – from a march, or a mass, or a dance – is dangerously overexciting: 'In China, music's an affair of state.'* In this way, Tolstoy is both *taking music in deadly earnest, and also identifying the extraordinary thing that has happened to music in Western culture, the essence of classical music in its purest form: that it is, so to speak,* just *music.*

Over the past few years I have had a number of residencies at concert halls in Europe and America. One of the most overwhelming concerts was one in which I played no part, beyond suggesting the programme and bringing the players together. At the Schubertiade in Schwarzenberg, the violinist Kathy Gowers and the pianist Julius Drake played the Beethoven 'Kreutzer'; the German actor Christoph Bantzer performed his own redaction of the Tolstoy story (which was indeed originally planned as a dramatic monologue); and the Belcea Quartet performed Janáček's quartet. The pieces followed each other directly – attacca *as we say in music, appropriately enough. Multiple reflections lit up the pieces from every angle and an unsettling emotional intensity was generated. It was as if these works should be heard only in this way, make sense only like this, a sense difficult to put into words, a musical sense that absorbs the literary and reacquaints it with itself.*

October 2008

We are living in an age that has seen the canon, in all the arts, disputed and undermined; in which the notions of aesthetic judgement and excellence have been contested; and in which the very notion of taste, crucial to the relationship between an artist and his or her public, has been mocked and corrupted to within an inch of its life.

The work of the French sociologist Pierre Bourdieu (who died in 2002), modishly impenetrable but essentially simple in its central assertion about cultural formation, has been extraordinarily influential here. Taste, he held, 'functions as a sort of social orientation, a "sense of one's place", guiding the occupants of a given social space towards the practices or goods which befit the occupants of that position'. His theory is based in empirical observation, and we know very well that the taste for cultural goods is socially stratified and inculcated in early childhood.

This shouldn't really make any difference to the status of the arts as sources of wisdom or enlightenment. They can be judged for what they have to offer, regardless of the origins of those who create or consume them, as natural science can. But the notion that the 'high' arts can be used as a buttress for social authority has radically undermined the legitimacy of judgements of cultural value in a democratic age. It makes us uncomfortable.

Here in Britain and America, we see the effects of this most clearly in music. One can argue very strongly that classical music is not in decline, that more people are listening to classical music than ever before, that the phenomenon of the ageing audience is a mirage (classical concerts have always been grey-headed affairs). It is undeniable, though, that classical music has lost the social authority that it had in its golden age. To put it at its most cynical, people no longer have to pretend to like it, or make an effort to like it in order to qualify as 'people of quality'.

Classical music reeks of class while at the same time classic rock rears its populist head. Politicians construct their cultural image around popular music – rubbing shoulders with Bono or filling their imaginary desert islands with the noises, sounds and sweet airs of gangsta rap and heavy metal (David Cameron on Radio 4).

The ironies are extraordinary, and not at all sweet. We are living in an age transfixed by the dystopian vision of a broken society, whose anxious leaders, to the Left and the Right, immerse themselves (or pretend to – and which is worse?) in a pop culture, much of which celebrates violence and drug-taking, and which is historically and aesthetically grounded in the tastes and predilections of the teenager. What is more, the whiff of rebellion on offer is a synthetic one, manufactured by gargantuan media companies for which this art (some of which, I stress, undoubtedly deserves this label) is a commodity.

Rock and roll is the art-form of late capitalism. It is not a utopian alternative to it or a protest against it. An early indication of this was the failure of the Beatles' utopian schemes for their Apple Corps in the late 1960s. 'A beautiful place where you can buy beautiful things . . . a controlled weirdness . . . a kind of Western communism,' as Paul McCartney called it. 'We're in the happy position of not needing any more money. So for the first time, the bosses aren't in it for profit. We've already bought all our dreams. We want to share that possibility with others.'

The corporation was most recently in the news settling a long-running trademark dispute with the Apple computer company. Bob Dylan's enlistment in a campaign for Victoria's Secret underwear was only the latest manoeuvre in this retreat from idealism.

For me, as a classical musician performing mostly repertoire that – unlike, say, Italian opera – has always been strictly segregated from and is difficult to assimilate to the pop tradition, the cultural sidelining of classical music is more than a little unsettling. So often there seems to be a need to explain or even apologise. Classical musicians seem ever eager to convince that the music they perform is interesting, relevant . . . groovy? It doesn't really convince anyone.

Pop music is pop music, creatively dominated by the model of the three- to four-minute song, even when it seeks to break out of those confines. It can be harmonically, rhythmically intriguing, and enthusiasts are forever pointing to this song in 5/4 time, or to that weird modulation, or rhapsodising about the final rising cacophonic crescendo at the end of *Sgt Pepper* culminating in a throbbing E major chord. But the best of the Beatles was pop simplicity – 'Yesterday', 'Norwegian Wood', 'Drive My Car' – rather than pop-art tricksiness.

Classical music, by the same token, is classical music. Ever influenced by popular styles and popular melody – Schubert and the Viennese waltz, Brahms and the *alla zingarese* style of Hungarian refugees in Hamburg, Thomas Adès and the club scene of the early twenty-first century – classical music yet remains essentially discursive, long-breathed, temperamentally serious, historically avant-garde. Though there may be all sorts of exceptions, we do violence to the aesthetic and historical facts if we pretend otherwise.

Just the other day I read an article in the *London Review of Books* by Nicholas Spice that bound together the recent case of Elisabeth Fritzl, the Austrian woman imprisoned for twenty-four years in a basement by her own father; the sadistic imaginings of Elfriede Jelinek, the one-time piano prodigy and Nobel Prize-winning Austrian novelist; and the privileged role of classical music in Austrian culture. I spend much of my professional life in Austria, a country where the classical musician can feel a little more at home. Here – for all sorts of reasons, historical, economic and cultural, some of them worthy, some less so – classical music is indeed culturally central, whether in the day-by-day bourgeois life of Vienna or in the hyper-reality of the Salzburg Festival.

It may not be good for one's moral health, this feeling of inflated significance, but it doesn't half soothe the bruised ego of the *soi-disant* serious musician. Yet Spice wants us to believe that Jelinek's experience, as a teenage pianist who had to escape the overbearing demands of the classical vocation pressed on her by her mother, tells us something sinister about classical music. 'Classical music', he writes, 'is always acceptable to authority, because it cannot overtly challenge power with subversive ideas or disturbing representations.'

The historical validity of this is immediately questionable: classical music has often challenged, disturbed and subverted. But I would argue that even today – in a subtle way, in the face of commodified popular music that sells itself as rebellion – the inner-directed seriousness of the classical tradition, compromised though it can be by hype and glitz, still presents a challenge to the way we live now.

One of the solaces for the musician abroad in the age of the Internet is to conjure away homesickness and ennui by tuning in to BBC Radio 4, live or as a podcast. The quarter-hourly chimes of Big Ben which kept me fitfully awake when I arrived, thirteen years old, at a boarding school next to Westminster Abbey, have mutated into the nostalgic charms of The World Tonight, *a news programme whose signature is Big Ben bonging (as one of my school-friends put it); the leaden circles, as Virginia Woolf put it in* Mrs Dalloway, *dissolve in the air. Melvyn Bragg's history-of-ideas strand,* In Our Time, *is, according to Will Self, required 'dilettante' listening. Laurie Taylor's* Thinking Allowed *presents the latest sociological research – often gleaned directly from the journals – through the crucible of Taylor's engaging radio persona. Not long after I had written the previous piece, Taylor's programme drew my attention to the latest piece of Bourdieu-inflected cultural sociology:* Culture, Class, Distinction, *a multi-authored study of the relationship between cultural practice and social stratification in contemporary Britain, published in 2009. It was a revelation to me, partly because I had thought of Bourdieu as just another one of those French intellectual gurus – Derrida, Foucault, Barthes – none of them noted for their immersion in nitty-gritty empiricism. This volume is, on the contrary, impressively founded in fieldwork that is statistically grounded, but also qualitatively presented, as we eavesdrop on hilarious conversations about cultural taste:*

SPUD: I love classical.
TOM: He's taking the piss. [General laughter]
MODERATOR: Nobody you particularly like, Spud?
SPUD: [pause]

BIF: He doesn't know a bloody name of a classical, that's what's wrong with him! [General laughter] But I am into it a bit. You wouldn't believe how much it gets the women going.

TOM: The what going?

BIF: The women going.

MODERATOR: But that's not perhaps the only reason you're into it . . .

DEN: You lying bastard.

BIF: No, not at all.

As so often in anthropological encounters, the subjects seem to have one over the investigator.

One of the book's major contentions is that music is 'the most divided [and] contentious' of all the cultural fields surveyed by the authors. If so, it must surely be because music is still so bound up with narratives of class and the ideology of social democracy. Rock music is the denim of musical fashion, stuck in a middle-class fantasy of identification with the ordinary worker. It remains, then, one of the cultural vestiges of the old Cold War polarities, which opposed a thriving, modern, rebellious, supposedly proletarian, and essentially American youth culture to the gerontocracy over the wall, the worker's state pickled in nineteenth-century bourgeois aesthetics. But, in the same way that you can now buy jeans on Bond Street for a few hundred quid, rock music has conquered the political and social elites, while retaining its often bizarre claim to authenticity.

There is a huge social and corporate investment in continuing to believe that rock music is countercultural and on the side of the angels, while the serious music of the past is stuffy and class-bound. The suggestion, as our authors have it, that classical music continues to 'evoke . . . hierarchy and power: the ghostly memories of legitimate cultural capital' is spot on. Evocations of the ghostly and not much more. It is the historian Tim Blanning who has underlined in his book The Power of Music *quite how powerful music has become in the postmodern age. But it's not the old music of the courts, salons and concert societies; it's the commodified music of the modern rock bands that buys musicians entry to No. 10 Downing Street, Davos and the G8. The bad conscience of a triumphant Western bourgeoisie and its service sectors is soothed by a music that manages to present hedonistic consumption in the trappings of nineteenth-century bohemianism and to absorb and redeploy the music of the dispossessed.*

The authors talk about those who enjoy rock and contemporary popular music 'narrat[ing] accounts of engagement, and excitement, which draw like-minded enthusiasts together in relatively exclusive groups'. This is something Simon Frith celebrates in his marvellous study of evaluation in popular music, Performing Rites, *a seductive vision of a democratic aesthetic, and one that undoubtedly reflects something of how people respond to the vast range of pop musics. Where the authors of* Culture, Class, Distinction *fall down, though, is in their rather thin account of engagement with classical music, which leads me to think that they may be as ignorant about it as I am about rock. To write that 'classical music . . . does not generate such excitement, but, especially for elite groups, it provides repertories and an arena for socialising' is a manifestly inadequate interpretation of either the inner-directed focus of a chamber-music performance or the electric excitement of the Simón Bolívar Youth Orchestra: like swordfighting, my eight-year-old son called it – wham, bam, wham.*

At the same time, the statistics in the book shake up some of our assumptions about musical taste. 15 per cent of the sample liked rock very much indeed, while 29 per cent did not like it at all; a comparable 16 per cent like classical music very much indeed while 23 per cent do not like it at all. Classical music turns out to be the single most popular genre, and 42 per cent of the sample responded to it positively. Quintessentially popular genres – urban, world, jazz, electronic music and heavy metal – have high negative ratings. And looking at responses to individual works, 56 per cent had listened to and liked Vivaldi's Four Seasons, *a score exceeded only by Sinatra's version of 'Chicago' at 65 per cent – Oasis, Eminem and Britney Spears tracks all scored lower on the listened to and liked test.*

November 2008

After my dyspeptic middle-aged rant last month about the hegemony of pop music and its teenage values (Disgusted of Tunbridge Wells my wife called it, but I stand by every word), it was nice to perform *Don Giovanni* to a Royal Opera House full of children and teenagers a few Thursdays ago, and to find it the most enlivening and inspiring experience. Instead of the normal general rehearsal in the morning – more or less thickly populated by relatives, friends of the house and so on – we played to a seething, cheering, booing, gobsmacked crowd of schoolchildren from sixty-eight different schools who filled the red-plush house to its rafters. Or so it seemed to me. That they should be amazed by the display of sophisticated pyrotechnics that Francesco Zambello's production conjures up for Don Giovanni's descent into hell was hardly surprising. That a sentimental (in the best sense) and understated masterpiece of stillness like the aria 'Dalla sua pace' would be attentively listened to and enthusiastically received was, however, reinvigorating.

The innocence of an audience of children is at one and the same time a little threatening and an opportunity. Art is artifice: contrived, artificial, mannered and, very often, an acquired taste. Performing something as apparently highfalutin as a Mozart opera, a canonical work if ever there was one, you are protected by the reverence that it holds around itself as an aura.

And the worry with an audience that doesn't bring that reverence is that the emperor will be found to have no clothes. Every sung performance in my experience has that quality of the best stand-up comedy – of teetering on the edge, of daring to be almost but not quite ridiculous – and children will not be too polite to laugh or yawn or fidget. Grown-ups, as concert- and opera-goers well know, tend to cough instead: mostly just as evident a sign of boredom and drifting attention, but one that is (on the whole) graciously afforded a viral alibi.

At the same time, the children who come to schools' matinées at the Royal Opera House are well prepared by their teachers – something we'd all love to do when we go to a show, but which we often forgo for lack of time – and they don't come with the negative baggage of thinking that 'something Great is something Boring'. They take it as it is, and if everyone singing and playing gives of their best, and gives generously and authentically, they will be drawn into unselfconscious enjoyment.

Children as audiences of sophisticated art-works are one thing. The aesthetic use of the child, and of childish innocence, within complex works of art, on the other hand, is something that can make us uncomfortable (think Balthus or Nabokov), especially when, as in the performing arts, the children in question are actually present.

There is a sort of two-track process going on when rehearsing a piece like Britten's operatic masterpiece, *The Turn of the Screw*, a consciousness among the adult per-

formers that while they themselves are engaging with inti-
mations of depravity, the children have to be shielded from
too much sense of what is going on. The same is surely
true in the final scene of Berg's *Wozzeck*, in which a small
child hears the news of his mother's death from a group of
his friends – to the accompaniment of obscenely mocking
woodwind – who then run off to view the body while he
remains innocently playing. 'Hop, hop,' he sings.

Britten learnt more from *Wozzeck* than any other single
piece – it informs the whole premise of *Peter Grimes*, the
shocking focus on a poetic brute, and saturates *The Turn
of the Screw*. His deployment of the child's perspective
throughout his oeuvre owes a huge amount to this devastating final scene – a far more interesting way of looking at
Britten's artistic practice than shamefaced imputations of
paedophilic scandal. In his *War Requiem*, a work as much
about death itself as about war, we confront the implac-
ability of death through the voices of children, who in their
rough simplicity (singing low in the voice, somewhat gruff-
ly) ask all too unknowingly, hence almost callously, for the
souls of the faithful to be delivered from the pains of hell,
the bottomless pit, the jaw of the lion. *Ne absorbeat eas tar-
tarus, ne cadant in obscurum* (neither let them be swallowed
up by Hell nor fall into darkness). Adult concerns voiced in
childish innocence – a potent device.

Last things in art are something I've been thinking about
more than usual over the past few months, performing in
recital and recording in the studio Schubert's last song-cycle,
Schwanengesang – 'Swansong', his publisher's posthumous
title. It's rather a mystery piece, with two groups of songs:
seven settings of Ludwig Rellstab and six of Heinrich Heine,

apparently disconnected but which the composer chose to write out as a single sequence in manuscript. In performance, despite all the theories of musicologists over the years, the manuscript order and single span of thirteen songs seem to make a sublime (if difficult to pin down) aesthetic unit.

But *Schwanengesang* as printed in 1828 consists of fourteen, rather than thirteen, songs, and not just because the publisher Tobias Haslinger was superstitious. He added, as a postscript or envoi, Schubert's very last song: the charming, lilting 'Die Taubenpost' (The Pigeon-Post), a poem by Johann Gabriel Seidl. In doing so, he offered us a vision of two sorts of sublimity. Late works, as John Updike has put it, 'exist, as do last words, where life edges into death, and perhaps have something uncanny to tell us'. Just as children offer a prospect of authenticity, so too do those at the end of life. Everything Schubert wrote after 1823, when he was diagnosed with syphilis and faced the prospect of insanity and death, constitutes late work.

The Heine settings of *Schwanengesang*, in their awful simplicity and starkness, in their radical subversion of the melodic impulse, offer one approach to encroaching finality. They still shock and they seem to reach far beyond the poems of lost love upon which they hang.

Yet Schubert's hauntingly melodic and wistful 'Taubenpost' seems to encompass a pulling-back from pessimism, cosmic or otherwise, and an embrace of life's rich if melancholy dance.

December 2008

As I write this piece, I'm about to set off on a tour of Japan, singing six recitals in two weeks: a biennial event for me, and one I used to dread. My first visit was to sing the small role of Sellem the auctioneer in Stravinsky's *Rake's Progress* at Seiji Ozawa's Saito Kinen festival in Matsumoto in 1995. In a provincial Japanese town for five weeks, arriving incongruously in the middle of a large Sumo wrestling convention, underemployed, phoning home infrequently (far too expensive) – I didn't embrace the experience but hunkered down in a faceless Hilton hotel clone, eating pizza and rereading Jane Austen.

Each subsequent visit has been easier, and performing to Japanese audiences is one of the great pleasures of my professional life. First and foremost, they know and love the repertoire I sing. There's an extraordinary and superficially surprising fit between Japanese musical tastes and Lieder, or German art-song as the Americans rather self-consciously call it. Audiences are concentrated, and know the words of the songs so well that they can often be seen (and remember, if you're ever in a Lieder audience, *we can see you*) mouthing them. The cultural fit is, of course, easily explained. German Romanticism had an enormous impact on Japanese thinking at the turn of the twentieth century, and an aesthetic of miniaturism is predisposed to appreciate an art-form one of whose primary exponents, Hugo Wolf, celebrated its smallness: 'Auch kleine Dinge können uns entzücken' (Small things can also delight us) is the opening song of his *Italienisches Liederbuch*, published in the 1890s.

Only a few years before I first went to Japan I was working in television, making business and politics programmes, and the Japanese economic miracle was the wonder of the world. We were desperate to churn out proposals for programmes about Japan, and the channels were desperate to commission them.

As I remember it – and were we not a little suspicious even at the height of the mania? – the grounds of the Imperial Palace in Tokyo were notionally valued as real estate at more than the entire state of California. Japanese political stability, the unique structure of Japanese conglomerates, the co-operative nature of Japanese management methods – these were all envied and discussed in think-tanks and policy forums in the West. Then came the bursting of the asset bubble and more than a decade of economic under-performance. The Nikkei index reached a high of nearly 40,000 in 1989. By 2003, when it finally started to rise again, it was at around a fifth of that level. It still stands at 9,000.

Which answers, I suppose, some of my selfish anxie-ties about the financial and economic crisis in which the world now finds itself, thanks to a bubble that has yet to be thoroughly anatomised. That is to say: life carries on, classical music still happens, I've been going regularly to Japan during the so-called 'lost decade' of economic stag-nation. And of course, in my world, while the cancella-tions have already started – especially of the big or risky projects in opera or symphonic touring – there's a feeling that serious music for serious times is something that will, relatively, prosper. Think the spirit of the Blitz, Myra Hess at the National Gallery. It's the same vague feeling that surrounded the Obama campaign, despite its messianic hoopla, that serious times demanded a serious, thoughtful, intellectual incumbent. But in the end, who knows? We're all guessing.

I like to feel that I'm full of insight about all this. I do remember sagely pointing out on the radio in November last year the cyclical nature of economic development, and the inability of markets ever to learn from history. However, the first ructions at Northern Rock had already happened by then, there was much more than a hint of trouble brewing and, crucially, very few of us, however much we see a crash coming, can extricate ourselves from our decade-long involvement in that bubble through our houses and our small-time investments. We are all, with very rare exceptions, materially but also psychologically implicated, and that is the lesson of history.

There is no question that the capacity of financial markets to turn nasty and present themselves with all the irresistible and apparently natural force of a hurricane or an earthquake – and these are the metaphors that we tend to use – is a compelling illustration of Marx's notion of alienation. We take human desires and needs, and progressively abstract and denominate them, freeze them – as money, stocks, futures, the whole range of complex derivatives – and they then turn against us with all the fury of a Golem.

This is something that those who were in on the first stirrings of modern financial markets already worried about. Daniel Defoe, trader, novelist and journalist, didn't only detect the 'villainy of stockjobbers', he also saw something Other and diabolical in the new, disembodied practices on Exchange Alley in the late seventeenth century. It was tantamount to witchcraft: what was real, men's goods and honour, was rendered imaginary; and what was imaginary, the current price of stocks, became real. Apparitions were conjured up, imaginations manipulated, with the 'strange and unheard of Engines of *Interests, Discounts, Transfers, Tallies, Debentures, Shares, Projects* and the *Devil and all* of Figures and hard Names'.

Performing the riches of the past, one is always looking for new ways to bring them alive to oneself and to the audience. I sang *Winterreise*, Schubert's great cycle of twenty-four Lieder to poems by Wilhelm Müller, last month in the Barbican – in the heart of the City of London – and one of the songs struck me with a new force. 'Im Dorfe', in the village, the wanderer, a loner, an outsider, rejected in love and rejecting bourgeois society, hears dogs bark and chains rattling and imagines the sleepers inside in bed: 'träumen sich Manches, was sie nicht haben, / Tun sich im Guten und Argen erlaben: / und morgen früh ist Alles zerflossen' (dreaming of much that they don't have, delighting in good things and bad, and early in the morning it has all melted away). The bubble-bursting flourish with which Schubert brings that phrase to an end says it all – the bourgeois dream and its inevitable evaporation.

Ironically enough, the world financial crisis brought me another Winterreise. *In 2009 across-the-board cuts in Italian arts budgets imposed by the Berlusconi government meant that the Maggio Musicale in Florence, one of the great music festivals of the world, had to cancel most of its opera programme at only a few months' notice. Instead of Verdi's* Macbeth, *we staged* Winterreise, *for one night only, in the vastnesses of the Teatro Communale. The director was the Italian movie maker Roberto Andò, who was to have undertaken the Verdi, and had longed to put* Winterreise *on stage. It was a fascinating experiment, and one that I could have undertaken only with my regular collaborator Julius Drake. We've performed the piece dozens of times and know each other's musical instincts backwards. Since I was often singing twenty or thirty feet away from him, this was, to say the least, a help. I ranged around an installation-cum-set, barefoot, lit, creating a trajectory for my wanderer, standing on chairs, on the edge of the stage, lying on my back, all manner of dramatic but improvised attitudes – opera but not opera. This is a way of excavating Schubert's dramatic impulse – best exemplified by his song-cycles rather than his operas, just as Handel's oratorios exhibit Handelian theatre at its most powerful – which reveals without destroying. In the end, we can go back to the simpler form, just singer and piano, with our instincts honed as audience member or performer.*

January 2009

Longer periods away from home – just over two weeks in Japan and Korea in this case – always make me think about time and our experience of it. On the larger scale, one experiences the elasticity of time complicated by homesickness, jet lag, work schedule and the personal, emotional shape of absence (the last couple of days always fly by as far as I am concerned). On the smaller scale, trips away are almost the only periods in which I experience regular, abstract exercise, usually swimming. If I swim twenty minutes a day for a week or more, the weirdness of time very quickly becomes apparent: the subjectivity of the time I experience, weaving in and out of my thoughts, is totally at odds with the stop-clock ahead of me, ticking away the seconds, and the ordinary clock to my left or right, converting time elapsed into portions of a circle, slices of a pie.

This is, it might seem, pretty banal stuff. The subjectivity of our experience of time is widely acknowledged. As we get older, time seems to go faster – or is it that we seem to move faster in time? The spatial images we use are confused and confusing. The theories to explain this change range from the physiological (the body cools as we age) to the arithmetical (each moment is a smaller proportion of a lengthening lifespan).

If time is so mutable, so much a matter of the ebb and flow of consciousness, is it in fact illusory? The common-sense view has long been that of classical science. Isaac Newton contrasted 'absolute, true, and mathematical time', which 'in and of itself and of its own nature, without reference to anything external, flows uniformly and by another name is called duration', with what he called 'relative, apparent and common time'. This is the view he bequeathed to the industrial age, the world of clocks, measurement and effective time management, but one that was exploded in its metaphysical aspects by Einstein's musings on relative motion and the speed of light, by the space–time continuum, and the uncertainties of quantum mechanics.

Time is the stuff of music: music manipulates our experience of time; it plays with the rhythm of experience; it stretches and complicates our relationship to the passing of time. If the world of physics is a space–time continuum, music is a pitch–time continuum. We use spatial metaphors to express our experience of frequency – notes are higher and lower, something expressed formally in staff notation, and deeply inscribed in our experience of music as performers and listeners. A large interval between two notes is a gulf to be stretched over. The quintessential musical form, melody, as it moves up and down in pitch-space, over time, is a sort of quasi-miraculous bridging of the gap between the abandoned past, the ungraspable present and the as-yet-to-be-achieved, utterly unreal future. We grasp it and, as we do so, time is attended to and made palpable and affective.

It's no coincidence that the great age of music as meta-physics – Schopenhauer above all – coincided with the construction of larger and more complex forms in classical music. These brought a specialised form of rationality, musical rationality, to the subjective experience of time, through both the eked out, endless melody of Wagner, and the great symphonic structures of Bruckner and Mahler. Nineteenth-century music's ambitions for itself were in many ways as cosmic as the Pythagorean vision of an art-form in tune with the construction of the universe, the music of the spheres. It wanted to mirror the ebb and flow of being itself.

While this all seems impossibly grandiose in a post-modern age, classical music still has the capacity to generate visions of the sublime. Here is Daniel Barenboim, recently quoted in the *International Herald Tribune*:

Since every note produced by a human being has a human quality, there is a feeling of death with the end of each one, and through that experience there is a transcendence of all the emotions that these notes can have in their short lives; in a way, one is in direct contact with timelessness.

There does seem a sort of affinity here between musical ambitions and the kind of metaphysics disdained by Anglo-American analytic philosophers. Karl Jaspers (1883–1969), for example, wrote of the possibility of certain experiences as 'instants of eternity in time', of a human capacity to be transported to an eternal present. Surely music might be one of these routes to epiphany?

The problem in Barenboim's analysis, though, is the very humanity of the musical experience he identifies. Because surely, when we get metaphysical about music, what we are looking for is an escape from ourselves, a direct glimpse of something transcendental, something objective if inchoate, a grappling with time and timelessness, with being and not-being, which goes beyond the messy subjectivity of our day-to-day perceptions and our all-too-limited language. We still long to grant musical discourse a special relationship with the world, we hanker after the music of the spheres. 'Such harmony', Lorenzo says to Jessica in *The Merchant of Venice*, 'is in immortal souls; / But whilst this muddy vesture of decay / Doth grossly close it in, we cannot hear it.' Romanticism's claim for our musical tradition is that in it, we hear some echo of the cosmos.

In the baldest sense this is pretentious nonsense. Music is a language, with a syntax that, whether generated by culture or embedded in our genetic make-up – or, most likely, a combination of both – is just as bound to us, to our humanity and our limited cognition, as ordinary language. There is no magical escape from the bounds of the human, from the veil of unknowing, the bonds of time.

And yet: in the same way that the metaphysicians – Schopenhauer, Heidegger, Jaspers – try to approach the unsayable and the unknowable, to break out of the limits of language and give at least an inkling, however illegitimate an inkling, of the nature of being and time (and I have to say that their attempts have never persuaded me, not that I'm a philosopher), music grapples with the sublime and the transcendent. In doing so it uses a language that, in its very lack of a proper semantics, its lack of definition, its continual striving to speak without actually speaking (or in the case of vocal music, saying so much more than is actually said), reaches outside itself more credibly than the jargon of the philosophers.

February 2009

Generally speaking, as a performer, even more as a classical singer, it is bad form to reply to criticism. The very personal nature of stage performance – the presentation of some version of the self, however well hidden or transformed – elicits a sort of visceral response from the critic. Trying to excuse one's perceived inadequacies or point out something crucial that has been missed or misunderstood seems rather beside the point and even impertinent. All performers, unless they live in a Xanadu world of *Citizen Kane*-like reclusiveness, will sometimes (or frequently) read reviews. But on the whole, we pretend that we don't, for the sake of our dignity. We also insist that the ultimately unmediated encounter with the audience is paramount.

With the written word it's a different matter, and having had an unusually large response on the *Standpoint* website to my last column, I thought I might clarify it just a little. I imagine that the interest was partly because the subject, our experience of time, is such a fascinating one, and one about which we all have something to say; but also because it is an area in which debate among professional philosophers is intense, often partisan and bewilderingly inconclusive. I was surprised, maybe even flattered, to have my scattered remarks analysed – mostly disparagingly, it has to be said – as philosophy.

Having been brought up close to the analytical tradition – two close school-friends have become philosophers, one working initially in the philosophy of science, the other in metaethics – sceptical of the metaphysicians, wary of the transcendental, I don't really believe that music does the work of metaphysics in any rationally engageable way. It is rather that in gesturing towards the unsayable – incoherent efforts as far as the analytical philosopher is concerned – music seems to me to do a more convincing job than the mystagogues of Paris and Frankfurt. What we cannot speak about, as Wittgenstein realised in his late philosophy, we do not pass over in silence, but endlessly mull over in art, religious doctrine and, perhaps above all, music. What is extraordinary is the continuing pertinence of the Romantic era's vision of musical transcendence to our own age. 'Music', as Beethoven had it, 'is the one incorporeal entrance into the higher world of knowledge which comprehends mankind but which mankind cannot comprehend.' True or not, we are still in thrall to such aspirations.

This month, I've been feeling distinctly corporeal. When all is well, singing is the sort of physical activity that brings with it a sense of release, of freedom and even exaltation. When all is not well (quite frequently), one feels the rustiness of the mechanism, its unwillingness to respond. Coax it like some temperamental engine and eventually it will kick into action. But when it comes to rather routine illnesses – in this case flu but more often a cold – things can seize up rather disconcertingly, a reminder of the brute materiality of what can seem a rather refined exercise.

To move from metaphysics to melancholia, as a singer it's not difficult to appreciate the relevance to daily and seasonal life of some skewed version of the old Galenic humoral theory, with its choleric, melancholic, sanguine and phlegmatic temperaments. My life is governed by phlegm to an extent that utterly disgusts my friends and family – even eight years of child-rearing have not desensitised my wife to this aspect of the human condition, and her opinion on the colour of the day's sputum is not usually canvassable.

The singer's slavery to even the most common of human ailments is difficult for the outsider to appreciate, so much so that when a singer has to cancel on account of the rhino-virus or one of its allies, the affliction being suffered is almost always beefed up to something more impressive-sounding. During the winter months, every day is spent anxiously reading the phlegmatic runes – steaming to ward off a viral threat, anxiously trying the voice out in the morning, try-ing to work out if that dry lack of suppleness is infective or due to over-enthusiastic central heating. Having an upper respiratory tract infection – and we singers feel every nook and cranny of the upper respiratory tract, from its top to its bottom, obsessively tracing the progress of the most subjec-tive sensations of infection – is for a singer the equivalent of pulling a muscle or a tendon for an athlete.

It makes us, despite the extrovert image of the opera singer, a very inward-looking breed, literally, obsessed with the health of tiny pieces of mucous membrane (the vocal cords) in the cartilaginous larynx, and of its surrounding tissue, all of it inside, and accessible only by the laryngo-scope (invented by a singer). Obsessive too. I shall never forget my wife returning home one afternoon to find me hunched over the computer, transfixed by what looked at first glance to be a rather unappetising pornographic web-site. In fact, battling my first bout of true laryngitis, the ultimate voice-killer, I was scanning endless close-ups of infected vocal tracts, trying to get a grip on my condition.

So I was prepared for the singer's experience of the coughs and sore throats that go with the flu: the irrational feeling that, however many times you've been through it before, this is the end. What I had forgotten was the overwhelming viral depression, which makes you wonder if you could be bothered even if the wretched voice did come back.

It is difficult to see the melancholy fit, when it is actually upon one, as creative; it saps action. Look at Dürer's female figure of melancholy, dark-faced, slumped, surrounded by all the instruments of creativity but unable to use them. Yet from the seventeenth century on, melancholy and creative frenzy were seen as intimately connected, part of the cultural construction that became the still reigning notion of the artistic genius. Beethoven is its prime exemplar: brooding and also, interestingly, dark-faced – a sufferer from the black bile, perhaps. Music retains a two-sided relationship to melancholia, both a curative, as David soothed Saul, and a quintessence, a sort of licensed wallowing. Or is it just playing at melancholy, perhaps, steeling oneself for its unpredictable, material descent? The Jacobean Robert Burton is the anatomist of all this, from the music that 'rears and revives the languishing soul', that which 'makes melancholy persons mad . . . the sound of those jigs and hornpipes . . . not [to] be removed out of the ears for a week after', to the music that causes a 'pleasing melancholy . . . [that] expels cares, alters . . . grieved minds, and easeth in an instant'.

I shall never forget a masterclass in which one of my fellow students proudly moved himself to tears with his own performance. The distinguished teacher's response was cruel but salutary: 'Don't worry, dear. It wasn't all that bad.' The relationship between emotion, art and performance is a tricky one. Music undoubtedly arouses emotion, but whether either the composer or the performer have to be in that emotional state to convey or incite it is doubtful. As a performer you can find yourself thinking about the oddest things, fleetingly, while delivering high emotion with a great deal of focus. That, I suppose, is what we mean by technique, and it is why actors, performing huge roles five times in the week and twice on a Saturday, can consistently and convincingly deliver without going doolally. It is very different for singers, who rarely perform more than three or four times a week at most. On the other hand I have given performances in a supercharged emotional state, convinced – like my friend above – that this inner state was inspiring a more engaged performance. This may or may not be true. I recently gave a performance of Mahler's 'Wo die schönen Trompeten blasen' from Des Knaben Wunderhorn, *where the pianist Julius Drake's playing of the opening* piano *lonely trumpet calls was so beautiful as to bring me to the verge of tears, something I had to struggle with for the rest of the song. At the apogee of nineteenth-century Romanticism, tears became part of the performing and audience experience, but for singers they cannot but be problematic, tending as they do to interrrupt breathing and phonation – in some senses a measure of how mannered a seemingly natural process must, in performance, be. Eighteenth-century commentators, anyway, were well aware of the distinction between an artistically effective assumption of melancholia, and the imbalance of yielding utterly to the thing itself. 'In languishing and sad passages,' writes C. P. E. Bach in his* Essay on the True Art of Playing Keyboard Instruments *of 1753, 'the performer must languish and grow sad . . . However, the error of a sluggish, dragging performance must be avoided, caused by an excess of affect and melancholy.'*

March 2009

After my battle with flu, I spent much of January and February in Deborah Warner's ENO production of Britten's last opera, *Death in Venice*, bringing it to La Monnaie in Brussels and the Grand Théâtre in Luxembourg. Reviving an opera production in which one has been deeply involved, eighteen months after its first outing, raises many issues, theatrical and otherwise.

As far as the design and technical crews are concerned, the change of venue is endlessly infuriating, as they try (and in the end, after long days and nights of tech-ing, succeed) to recapture the atmosphere conjured up by lines of sight, lighting cues, video installations and so on, in spaces that, on this occasion, were utterly different from the originating house. The London Coliseum is a big Edwardian variety theatre with a panoramic stage. La Monnaie is a classic late nineteenth-century opera house, smaller and rounder. The Grand Théâtre is a 1960s confection: multipurpose, small and without boxes.

In Luxembourg, the structure of the theatre was such that I – playing the long, complex and interior role of the frustrated literary lion, Gustav von Aschenbach – could see the faces of the audience (not so in Brussels or London) and hear every whisper in the wings, requiring a different sort of concentration and a different engagement with the public. Aschenbach's monologues, revealing the tortuous thought processes that he hides from the world around him, are very different in character when you see the audience, for obvious reasons. I am reminded of Fintan O'Toole's brilliant dissection of Shakespearean soliloquy, his realisation that the notion of talking to yourself is not part of

Elizabethan theatrical practice, that when Hamlet says 'To be or not to be' he is self-consciously, naturally, engaging the audience, like a stand-up comic, a world away from the misty pieces to camera in Laurence Olivier's film version.

Rehearsing for a revival brings new discoveries, but the recovery of familiarity comes first. The practical, apparently trivial details that determine much of the emotional contours of a performance – move downstage here, pick up the notebook at the end of suppertime, smoke a Toscana cigar at this point rather than a cigarette – are semi-enshrined in the assistant's score, and often impossible to pick out with any exactitude from the darkly lit reference video which was often made before the show had reached crystallisation. Yet what I realised, despite my self-caricature as a disembodied type, an intellectual performer, is that after a proper period of rehearsal and immersion in a role which one at the same time invents and discovers, the moves and rhythms of the performance are written in the body as much as the music is programmed into the vocal muscles. The sensations and nuances flood back.

There were changes. In 2007 I grew a Thomas Mann lookalike moustache which my wife and children rather took against. This time, I somewhat ineffectually sprouted a grizzled and greying beard that had even more of the ageing effect the costume designer Chloë Obolensky was aiming for. The impact of actually growing the beard or moustache, rather than wearing a false one, is important in terms of what one thinks acting actually is. For some, to act is a matter of impersonation – Olivier donning a putty nose for Richard III or a pair of false teeth for Shylock, or the increasing tendency in movies (the sort that used to be called biopics) for the actor to become unrecognisable in terms of accent, mannerism, physical build and so on. The transformation can be, is meant to be, astonishing, miraculous.

To make the simple transition from clean-shaven to bearded represents, on the other hand, in its very simplicity and subtle realism, a conception of acting as a matter of rehearsing and performing towards an accommodation between the character as presented in the text and one's own self. As I've already said, you invent and discover. My own experiences, tendencies, habits, moods and memories have to be subsumed into the journey from professional dignity, repression and order to the disorder, humiliation and transfiguration that are Aschenbach's in *Death in Venice*. That's why it is important to me that the novella and opera are not simply about a failing writer who falls inappropriately in love with a teenage boy. The impact of the story and the way it is told are far more universal. It's like Flaubert saying: 'I am Madame Bovary.' We are all Gustav von Aschenbach.

If December and the first half of January were spent fighting influenza, my time in Brussels and Luxembourg was all about pretending to do battle with cholera. Mann's title *Death in Venice* has three aspects: the death of Aschenbach himself; the uncanny personification of death in the strange figures who accost the writer during his reckless sojourn (a theme that the dying composer amplified to chilling effect in the opera); and the cholera that is rampaging through the city. It's often been thought that Mann was exaggerating the extent of the cholera on the 1911 trip that inspired the book, but in fact the last great cholera pandemic did reach Europe, Italy in particular, killing 116 people in Venice, 873 in Naples and 6,146 in the country as a whole. It inspired a government cover-up that threatened non-compliant doctors with jail and falsified the historical record.

Hanseatic, wealthy Hamburg (Thomas Mann was from neighbouring and Hanseatic Lübeck) had suffered a shocking outbreak only two decades earlier, 8,616 people dying of the disease in 1892. But cholera, over and above the historical account, is ideal for Mann's purposes in *Death in Venice*. Chillingly swift and undignified in its impact upon the human body, it is the master metaphor of the novella, its power as a metaphor only enhanced by the fact – one I took on board in the past month – that Mann is resolutely ambiguous as to whether Aschenbach actually dies of the disease. 'Disease', as Mann was to write in *The Magic Mountain*, 'is only love transformed' – and Aschenbach's sickness is really of the soul.

Britten and his librettist, Myfanwy Piper, brilliantly intensify this by getting Aschenbach to emphasise his thirst, his thirst for change, at the beginning of the opera – terrible thirst being, of course, one of the early symptoms of cholera. At this early stage, there can be no notion that he actually has the disease, but the lines are being blurred, in the same way that the smeary low tuba sonorities at the end of the act confuse and muddy the declaration of his secret love. Ambiguity is a feature of all Britten's operas, as he himself acknowledged, and it is a strangely unoperatic quality – one of the keys to his modernity, and unsettling. What I have yet to rationalise is how as an actor one can characterise that ambiguity. Does Aschenbach contract cholera? Do I need to know?

My point about schools of acting was nicely made by the bril-

liant theatre critic Paul Taylor in a piece about Simon Russell Beale I came across recently in the Independent:

The only actor who operates on the same plane of achievement as Russell Beale is Mark Rylance. The contrast between them reminds me of the distinction that Dr Johnson made between Milton and Shakespeare. Rylance is the Prince of the Protean. He's like Shakespeare who, chameleon-like, disappears into his characters ... Simon Russell Beale, by contrast, is more like Milton, who turns everything into the struggle of being Milton ... part of the joy of watching this actor is the sense that you are getting the latest instalment in the ongoing drama of being Simon Russell Beale.

April 2009

Music resounds through nineteenth-century fiction, high and low, as a measure of the ineffable, the spiritual, and the deep. Sherlock Holmes's musicality is a sure sign of his superior and mysterious intelligence. His friend Watson's slight philistinism in relation to Holmes's 'scraping upon the violin' becomes a clear marker of his role in the stories as what Americans call 'a regular guy'.

Less formulaically, and with a greater degree of thematic integration, George Eliot's last novel, *Daniel Deronda* (1876), is suffused with music as a symbol of a deeper current in life, significantly intertwined with its treatment of Jewish culture, politics and spirituality. Daniel Deronda, raised as an English gentleman, discovers that he is Jewish and marries the outcast Mirah Cohen. This is the countermovement in the novel to Gwendolen Harleth's failed experiment in marrying the sadistic Mallinger Grandcourt for power. Yet in choosing Mirah, Deronda also chooses a singer. In discovering his real mother, he finds her to have been a singer too, and a great one. Gwendolen's musical talent, displayed in the early chapters, is found to be superficial, a matter of appearances rather than true musicality. It is Klesmer, the superlative musician, who makes this judgement and whose proud if ever so slightly comic words in another scene confirm music as a central metaphor in the novel. 'I was sure he had too much talent to be a mere musician,' declares Mr Bult, who is 'an esteemed party man', to Klesmer.

'Ah, sir, you are under some mistake there,' said Klesmer, firing up. 'No man has too much talent to be a musician. Most men have too little . . . We help to rule the nations and make the age as much as any other public men. We count ourselves on level benches with legislators.'

After a break of a year or so, I'm starting to have singing lessons again (unique among musicians, most singers have teachers throughout their working lives). So I thought it would be fun to read the most famous book of all about a singer and a singing teacher, George du Maurier's *Trilby*, first published as a serial in 1893. If George Eliot's prose (I've just started rereading *Deronda*) is just occasionally overloaded by the effort to project intellectual respectability in the face of a rather scandalous life, du Maurier's book is a confection of the most appalling heartiness, its prose bespattered with exclamation marks – I swear there was a page on which every sentence ended with one! – and choc-a-bloc with toe-curling sentimentality: *La Dame aux camélias* meets *Three Men in a Boat*, without the brilliance of either. While much of the book concerns itself with evoking the bohemian milieu of three aspiring British painters in mid-century Paris – their parties, their dinners, their habits, their artistic talents and failings – it is the artist's model Trilby, a beautiful, captivating Irish girl, who gives her name to the book and gives it a focus. The great painter of the three, nicknamed Little Billee, falls hopelessly in love with her, but his mother intervenes and dissuades Trilby from marrying her son.

What lifts the book rather dubiously above this unpromising romance, and made it into one of the great phenomena of publishing history – a smash in America, a stage play, giving its name to the Trilby hat – was the creation of a sinister mesmeric musician, Svengali. Svengali's name has entered the language, a villain to rank with Count Dracula in the popular imagination. His magnetic powers make of Trilby – comically tone-deaf at the start of the novel – the greatest singer of the age, courted by the great and admired to distraction by the musical elite. Svengali's death during one of her performances leaves her bereft of her talent, a laughing stock, emptied out and destined to die.

It is an extraordinary invention, one with which du Maurier regaled his friend Henry James (always at a loss for plots) on one of their Hampstead walks. James noted it down as a possible idea for a novel of his own. How different that would have been; though the possession of one human being by another, the vampiric urge, is the melodrama that lies at the heart of a novel as subtle as *A Portrait of a Lady*.

With *Daniel Deronda* in mind, it's extraordinary to what extent *Trilby*, written nearly twenty years later, is an anti-*Deronda*. Eliot's sympathetic tapestry of musical and Jewish culture becomes in *Trilby* a hideous anti-Semitic fantasy, Svengali perhaps the most egregious example of the demonic Jew in English literature. The book has no clear programme and, at one level, it pays a heady tribute to the art of music. Little Billee, hearing Svengali play,

was conscious, while it lasted, that he saw deeper into the beauty, the sadness of things, the very heart of them, and their pathetic evanescence, as with a new, inner eye – even into eternity itself, beyond the veil – a vague cosmic vision that faded when the music was over, but left an unfading reminiscence of its having been, and a passionate desire to express the like some day through the plastic medium of his own beautiful art.

Yet it is the magic of music that is repeatedly stressed, both in the account of Trilby's exquisite *bel canto* – 'every separate note was a highly finished gem of sound, linked to the next by a magic bond' – and in the insistence on the power of music: 'It is irresistible; it forces itself on you.' And magic is ultimately the province of the sinister oriental, Svengali, 'a magician', the hypnotist, the entrancer.

What remains interesting for a musician today, and for a singer in particular, is *Trilby*'s relationship to Victorian efforts to understand what Herbert Spencer called 'The Origin and Function of Music' (an article he wrote in 1857). For Spencer (and we see his account reflected in du Maurier's evocations of Trilby's art), singing originated in reflex actions of the larynx, varied vocal responses to emotion which, received by a listener, elicited sympathy. 'These various modifications of voice became not only a language through which we understand the emotions of others, but also the means of exciting our sympathy with such emotions.' It is the intricate brocade of music woven from the primitive, instinctive response of our distant ancestors.

May 2009

Since I'm on a point-to-point tour in the US at the moment – zigzagging around the East Coast from New York to New Hampshire via Savannah, Boston, Baltimore and Princeton, New Jersey – my assembled thoughts may take on an even more rambling character than usual. Writing a column can induce a vertiginous sort of legitimation crisis – one's words, sentences and paragraphs are self-certifying, since the columnist can write pretty much whatever he or she fancies – and occasionally the terrifying spectre of block rears up. What shall I write about? Or, more often perhaps, what shall I not write about? For the professional writer, of course, it's much worse, the daily encounter with the blank sheet or screen. I've been reading a lot of Updike on the road or in the air – he's recently deceased and I'm in his neck of the woods – and have relished the following exchange between the fictional author Henry Bech and his current squeeze:

'You should get out of these dreary rooms, Henry. They're half the reason you're blocked.'
　'Am I blocked? I'd just thought of myself as a slow typist.'
　'What do you do, hit the space bar once a day?'
　'Ouch.'

So, to resume where I left off last month – singing teachers. After a gap of a few years – and some internal resistance – I have gone to a new teacher and it's been a revelation. Some of the discoveries have been matters of small physical adjustments, things that have a palpable effect on the ease or placing of a voice but which, once discovered, have to be worked on over weeks and months before they can become second nature. In the end, technique has to be subordinate to the music itself and its transmission, but achieving that is, of course, the hardest technical task of all.

My resistance may have been down to laziness or perhaps fear of the unfamiliar. One never wants to change what has been, or is still, working. But the problem is that it will not work indefinitely. Singers can have long careers and there are famous examples of those who performed well into old age. I remember hearing Alfredo Kraus sing a beautiful, believable Nemorino (essentially, a young man's role) in Donizetti's *L'elisir d'amore* in his late sixties. Hugues Cuenod, the Swiss tenor, 107 next month, was singing in public well into his eighties. Plácido Domingo is a marvel of longevity. But as we age, the body changes and the smart singer has to be ever alert to the physical adjustments needed to cope with minute shifts in stance, bearing or a host of other bodily biases.

More generally, though, I've never been easy with thinking about the voice as a physiological phenomenon. By which I mean that while recognising the voice as physical, I've always preferred to approach it through a veil of metaphor, the well-worn images of most vocal pedagogy: balls floating on jets of water; domes on the sound; spaces made in all sorts of places that exist only in the imagination. 'Support' is the thing all singing teachers agree on as the basis of sound technique, but no one seems to agree on where it is located or exactly what it is. The images are epiphenomena achieving real physical effects, which I am at a loss to understand physiologically, while realising all along that there must be a physiological explanation.

There's a vague parallel in philosophy of mind. Materialists – 99 per cent of the philosophical community, I would guess – are condemned in the bulk of their lives to using the mental categories of what they (disparagingly, it would seem) call 'folk psychology', while at the same time remaining convinced that there must be an, as yet unreachable, purely physical description.

A closer parallel exists in what one might call the philosophy of pianism, and one that raises a lot of hackles.

Charles Rosen, the pianist and peerless writer about music, strenuously maintains that the engineering of the piano precludes a whole host of things that pianists are taught to believe in, and centrally, the notion that a pianist can have such a thing as a 'touch'. As Rosen himself has put it:

You push a piano key down, and it is louder and softer, and longer and shorter. There is nothing else you can do to an individual note that makes the slightest difference to the music. It is the way the notes are combined by the pianist that makes a beautiful tone.

Yet, talking to pianists with whom I work, they are, regardless of Rosen's reasoning, absolutely committed to what must be, from a purely physical and mechanical point of view, a metaphorical way of thinking. Somehow, it helps to pretend that something is happening that can't be.

I've always realised that there is a physiological basis to vocal production, of course, while at the same time finding it too confusing an idea to handle in detail. Intellectually curious as I like to think I am, books about vocal physiology – rather like books about personal finance – have tended to confuse me and make me blurry-eyed. But now I'm going to a singing teacher who (and this is a rarity) works closely with a laryngologist and a physiotherapist, who can tell me things about the relationship between the various parts of the vocal mechanism without sending me into a Weberian tailspin. I think it was Max Weber who said that if you think about how to walk, you fall over.

My teacher's most interesting general point about the vocal mechanism is that, unlike the piano, it is not designed for the purpose with which we most associate it. The primary function of the vocal tract is as one of several lines of defence against choking, that elemental confusion of the

trachea and the oesophagus, the windpipe and the food-
pipe, a nasty consequence of the evolutionary economy of
the human animal. If I've understood him properly, much
of what we do as singers, particularly in achieving the high
notes that technique facilitates, is actually about persuading
the body that one is not about to swallow as one reaches for
the skies. And with that rather excruciating physical image
I leave you.

Updike's Rabbit *novels – the tetralogy plus valedictory novella
– are as marvellously depressing as his Henry Bech is funny.
We follow Harry 'Rabbit' Angstrom, the high-school basket-
ball star, an American Everyman, through four decades of an
American century, a snapshot of each (50s, 60s, 70s, 80s). I read
the four novels one after another in a matter of months in 2001
– what a year that was for America – and they did leave me
profoundly unsettled, a sort of mid-life crisis of novel-reading.
But, as has so often been pointed out, the paradox that stands at
the centre of the construction of the books – the finely honed,
sensitive, expressive and essentially literary sensibility possessed
by their ever-so-ordinary,workaday, often oafish protagonist –
is uplifting. The brilliance of the excavation of Harry's inner
life is dazzling, and Harry's possession, despite everything, of
this current of the extraordinary, is democratic in the best possible way, without being sentimental or unduly idealistic. 'The
motions of Grace, the hardness of the heart; external circumstances' (Pascal, Pensée 507): Updike's epigraph to the first of
the sequence,* Rabbit, Run. *What makes a life?*

*A jumble of reading and looking and listening feeds into my
work as a singer.* Winterreise *is a particular sort of journey,
rich in metaphor.* Rabbit, Run *is another. Reading Harry's
impulsive attempt to drive away from his settled bourgeois*

life at the beginning of Rabbit, Run *made me think, maybe implausibly, of a modern* Winterreise *in early spring. Harry sets off and manages to 'drive . . . forty miles to get sixteen miles away'. He wanders without a map. A petrol-pump attendant confronts him with the obvious and at the same time gnomic truth: 'The only way to get somewhere, you know, is to figure out where you're going before you go there.' Harry fails. He gives up on his aimless quest, goes back to his home town, and sets in train a series of events which end in appalling tragedy. At the end of the book, he's still on the run:*

Rabbit comes to the curb but instead of going to his right and around the block he steps down, with as big a feeling as if this little side-street is a wide river, and crosses. He wants to travel to the next patch of snow. Although this block of brick three-stories is just like the one he left, something in it makes him happy; the steps and window sills seem to twitch and shift in the corner of his eye, alive. This illusion trips him. His hands lift of their own and he feels the wind on his ears even before, his heels hitting heavily on the pavement at first but with an effortless gathering out of a kind of sweet panic growing lighter and quicker and quieter, he runs. Ah: runs. Runs.

June 2009

Benjamin Britten stands for two crucial things in the world of music. First and foremost is the music itself, which is unapologetically grounded in familiar diatonic harmony, resistant to the totalising claims of modernism. This is music, which *pace* Stravinsky, *can* express something; music that resists the youthful conviction of Pierre Boulez that 'any musician who has not experienced – I do not say understood, but truly experienced – the necessity of the dodecaphonic language is USELESS'. Stravinsky himself, the icon of classical music in the twentieth century – even the great and in many ways reactionary Stravinsky – lacked the confidence to resist this sort of aggressive appeal to the historical inevitability of tonal dissolution. The revolutionary potential of vanguardist music now reads, of course, like some sort of sick joke.

Britten's dramatic subjects, in opera and song, are often centred on ambiguity, which musical language, non-denotative as it is, is supremely well able to capture. But with Britten music, however difficult to pin down, however multifaceted and multivalent, was not just about itself, as Eduard Hanslick had claimed in the nineteenth century, as Stravinsky claimed in the twentieth. A supreme master of form, Britten was no formalist. To be suggestive, as his music so eminently is, is to suggest *something* after all. Britten remains one of the few masterly twentieth-century voices – Janáček, Sibelius, Bartók are some of the others – who were able to resist the siren call of new systems, of tone rows, or the alienated and alienating avant-garde. He proved that music written in the tradition of Bach, Mozart and Schubert, and using the same means as those composers, need not be either nostalgic kitsch or archly referential. The seam of invention was by no means exhausted. As a result, his music lives and is performed and appreciated worldwide.

If Britten stands out for his rejection of avant-gardism, that has to be seen in the context of a social philosophy of music. For him, music was linked to local purpose, to small enterprises, and he was suspicious of glamour and of fashion, and resistant to co-option in Vanity Fair, the musical merry-go-round. As Paul Kildea suggests in his contribution to the Boydell Press's handsome *New Aldeburgh Anthology*, the success of Britten's opera *Peter Grimes* weeks after the cessation of hostilities in Europe in 1945 gave him enormous credibility. A very British success in a hitherto Continental field of cultural endeavour meant that the composer had accumulated great cultural capital. Many would have spent this capital on feathering their nests in the metropolis. Britten, however, devoted his energies instead to a musical experiment in an out-of-the-way provincial locale. His reasons for doing so may have been as personal as they were idealistic. His homosexuality and his sensitivity to criticism – particularly after the scandalised reception of his Coronation opera *Gloriana* – were important factors in his retreat from mainstream cultural life. But the result has been, extraordinarily, to give a permanent place in the world's musical calendar to a tiny seaside town.

Aldeburgh started in 1948 as one of the many arts festivals that sprouted after the war – such as Edinburgh and Holland. Its ethos was 'small is beautiful' and an attempt to capture a Schubertian sense of friends making art together. It provided an arena for Britten premieres and for bringing together, in the context of a small Suffolk coastal town, some of the giants of the international music scene – Richter, Fischer-Dieskau, Rostropovich. There were community works to be done, and Britten engaged his full genius in writing them – think of his children's opera *Noye's Fludde* – but also first performances of works that have become repertory standards in the largest concert halls and theatres. I last saw Britten's *A Midsummer Night's Dream* in the vastness of the Metropolitan Opera (capacity four thousand), New York (population eight million). It is extraordinary to remember that it had its first performances in the Jubilee Hall (capacity three hundred), Aldeburgh (population three thousand). Today, the Aldeburgh Festival has developed beyond all measure in its ambitions, but the expansion of teaching, residencies and performance spaces has remained true to the localist ambitions of its founders. Aldeburgh now runs events throughout the year, and an exciting new performance space has just been opened. The Festival proper, the sixty-second, takes place this month.

Far away from all that, I have been singing Britten's Rimbaud cycle for string orchestra, *Les Illuminations*, in Chicago with Bernard Haitink and the city's magnificent Symphony Orchestra (conductor emeritus, the aforementioned Pierre Boulez). This is the other side of Britten, playing the international circuit, but it struck me forcefully that many members of the orchestra didn't really know the work beforehand and were blown away by it. It's a very American piece, completed while Britten was living in Amityville outside New York and with, indeed, a very Chicago vibe, full of musical and poetic images of city bustle – threat and opportunity – and the metaphorical presence of water, gleaming, glistening and slithering, to drown in and to dissolve our differences, our preconceptions. Water, the lake, is crucial to the character and the colour of Chicago.

If Britten's music is pretty unfamiliar territory for the orchestra here – Shostakovich, for example, is more their sort of thing (they were playing his last symphony as part of the programme, a piece they know well) – it's not entirely their fault. Britten didn't write many big symphonic works and used his unrivalled understanding of Mahlerian orchestration more often in the context of reduced, chamber-orchestra forces. Again, it's all of a piece with the philosophy, the preference for the small-scale, a sort of self-denying ordinance. What has kept Britten at the centre of the glamorous international musical machine has been the music theatre, the unrivalled achievement of a large body of singable, profound and original opera written in a period where some (Boulez again) were calling for the opera houses to be burnt down.

The week I sang *Les Illuminations*, Britten's pacifist opera *Owen Wingrave* was in rehearsal at the Chicago Opera Theater. The big question – and it is the same question I face every time I sing a Schubert song in Carnegie Hall, La Scala or the Barbican – is whether one can remain true to the genius of a chamber work like *The Turn of the Screw* or *A Midsummer Night's Dream* when producing it in a large house. It seems to me that it is only by moving back and forth between the local and the metropolitan or cosmopolitan that one can have any hope of keeping the spirit of the music alive. And in the end that is the artistic, rather than the political or social, rationale for the community and education work that is ever more important for opera houses and orchestras the world over.

The greatest social revolution to have happened in my lifetime has undoubtedly been the acceptance of homosexuality, both legally, and as a valid way of life in the mainstream of society, despite persistent pockets of homophobia. The relationship between Britten and Pears led the way in this regard, a gay marriage of hearts and minds that was accepted at the most exalted levels of British society long before the law changed, and in the face of an anti-gay campaign under a Conservative home secretary, Sir David Maxwell Fyfe, in the early 1950s.

A couple of days after filing this piece, I picked up the latest, second, volume of Isaiah Berlin's letters (Enlightening, 1946–1960) in Daunt's bookshop near the Wigmore Hall, skimming the index for anything that might immediately grab me. Britten was mentioned in two letters. Writing to his friend Rowland Burdon-Muller in August 1952 about an enjoyable trip to Aix-en-Provence, Berlin describes 'a great celebration of homintern'. Homintern was the homosexually inclined don Maurice Bowra's phrase, not an indicator of anti-gay prejudice, but Berlin clearly found composer and singer a dubious pair: 'Benjamin Britten + Peter Pears, an obvious ménage, appeared & he sang with a degree of sentimentality, deeply & sincerely in love with his own unbeautiful voice, which was embarrassing.' This to the (probably) gay interior designer, who had his own American ménage with the art collector Charles Hoyt. To Oliver Franks, a bastion of the Establishment if ever there was one, Berlin – whose intersecting social circles were a map of 1950s society, hence much of the interest of the letters – was much more forthright, less camp and teasing. Berlin was on the board of the Royal Opera and felt in July 1958 that Britten would be a bad choice as music director:

It is difficult to think of arguments against him, and he would certainly be a 'prestige' appointment and satisfy a section of the critics and the musicians; what I have against him is that he is part of the same gang as Webster and, not to put too fine a point upon it, opera is an essentially heterosexual art, and those who do not feel affinity with this tend to employ feeble voices, effeminate producers etc., which is a very large factor in our present misfortunes . . . Here is Britten, a composer of immense talent – whose music I do not greatly enjoy, though I admire it and am prepared to concede that he is a composer of genuine genius – who has at Aldeburgh created a kind of sweetly arty-crafty little Festival to which all the members of his 'persuasion' flock, and it has its own quality no doubt, but it would be hateful to see Covent Garden going that way – indeed it is far too much that way already. I wish I did not sound so much like Maxwell Fyfe. No doubt it will be thought unrespectable to oppose Britten.

There is much to enjoy and fascinate here, in terms both of unwitting comedy and of the complexities of sexual politics in this period, just after the Wolfenden report which had, the year before, recommended liberalising the laws on homosexual activity. But the idea of the Aldeburgh Festival as a 'kind of sweetly arty-crafty little Festival to which all the members of his "persuasion" flock' is a reminder of the deep reserves of English philistinism that could be drawn on even by as cultured and sensitive an individual as Berlin. It's a wonderful irony that, despite the condescension, this 'sweetly arty-crafty little Festival' has been an engine for some of the greatest music-making of the past sixty years, and an unparalleled arena for musical innovation to boot.

FUGITIVE NOTES

Authoritative Voices

Review of John Potter, *Vocal Authority*
and Hans Neunzig, *Dietrich Fischer-Dieskau: A Biography*
(transl. Kenneth Whitton)

We live in an age in which the role of classical music is in endless dispute; at the same time, the music itself has never been more listened to, or appreciated. Technical developments are largely responsible – the impact of recording has been vast and multifaceted. The drawbacks are familiar: the destruction of domestic music-making and the creation of a middle-brow market (in itself a good thing), together opening up a gulf between a musically illiterate audience and an increasingly self-conscious avant-garde; the threat to live music; the crisis of overproduction, with its glut of barely distinguishable recordings of the same pieces. The positive aspects are less often dwelt on: a rising standard of competence, even expressivity, among musicians; the success of the period-performance movement, despite all its philosophical absurdities; and an unparalleled availability to ordinary people of some of the greatest works of the human imagination. In the era of reproduction and remote-control experience, the live event may, contrary to the jeremiads, gain in appeal; there is no reason why recordings should not, as they already do, build up, rather than eat away at, audiences.

Political legitimacy is a different matter, as excellence, elitism and snobbery are confused, and the public provision of cultural excellence comes to be seen as some sort of middle-class scam. John Potter's study of 'singing style and ideology', *Vocal Authority*, is a fruit of this climate, worried as it is about the democratic legitimacy of mainstream classical singing. One of the appeals of the book is the deconstruction of that mainstream, with an attempt to place it on an expressive continuum with pop singing of various sorts. The problem is Potter's relentless use of sociological jargon, and his efforts to harness an analysis of singing styles to a clumsy marxisant account of (most of) European history.

Today, vocal authority certainly seems to be a disintegrating force. On my way past the Sony Centre in New York recently, I heard some familiar music being sung in a distinctly unorthodox way. The music was 'Nessun dorma', firmly associated in all our aural imaginations with Luciano Pavarotti; the disconcerting other voice was that of the pop singer Michael Bolton revealing his 'Secret Passion' in a disc just released by Sony, a disc that has sailed to the top of the specialist classical charts. Sony Classics is a significant force in classical music, the possessor of the riches of the CBS back-catalogue and responsible for the recent, very distinguished, recordings of Handel, Scarlatti, Schumann and Bach by the American pianist Murray Perahia. Here at the centre of the classical business, with apparently reckless concern for the 'purity' of the brand, was a 'rock' voice performing music written for an 'operatic' voice. It is earthy, rasping even, and doesn't defer to classical models of tonal beauty (the synthetic recording technique and reorchestrations are equally outside the classical orbit).

An earlier excursion into this sort of crossover (usually, it's classical artists being inadequate in jazz or pop music) constituted, bizarrely, my first experience of German song: Barbra Streisand's album of the 1970s, *Classical Barbra*, which CBS produced and Leonard Bernstein generously endorsed. This is often referred to as a successful album – I've even been told that the revered Dutch soprano Elly Ameling thought that it could teach mainstream classical singers a thing or two. To me it seems, on the contrary, that all Streisand's customary virtues, her engagement with a text and, above all, the passion of her voice, are repressed in the service of certainly pretty, but rather polite, over-careful and rhythmically boxed-in accounts of songs such as Schumann's 'Mondnacht' and Hugo Wolf's 'Verschwiegene Liebe'.

If this was the classical Barbra – intimidated into politeness – classical Bolton, twenty years on, represents another extreme: verismo bruised into submission. Vocal authority, along with the unquestioned status of the classical repertoire, has splintered. While the application of a quasi-operatic style to popular standards, so familiar a generation ago, now seems an embarrassment, pop singers no longer defer to a classical ideal. Whether this is part of a more general movement is not yet clear. Whether Bolton's high sales represent anything other than Bolton fans buying anything by Bolton, I don't know; whether the management at Sony Classical was leant on by Sony Music to indulge Bolton, I don't know either. But in terms of classical sales, it is certainly not always technical or expressive prowess, as defined by the elites of the profession (other singers, teachers, conductors, the cognoscenti), which rises to the top.

Marketing counts more than ever, as does media-friendly personality and popular taste. Boundaries are being broken. On the other hand, the most famous tenor in the world, Luciano Pavarotti, is undoubtedly, like the first media tenor star, Enrico Caruso, a prodigious figure as a singer, one who works within the traditional disciplinary boundaries of register, vibrato, colour, expression and line.

John Potter sets out to examine why singing styles come and go, and why particular styles are what he calls 'hegemonic', that is to say, authoritative at any one time within their milieu, and beyond. His theory of singing style is the familiar triad of innovation, dominance and decadence. Decadence spawns, in turn, fresh innovation.

For Potter, the driving-force behind innovation is the delivery of textual meaning, which is in turn subverted by technique. Thus, the 'speech-like declamation' of Louis Armstrong and Bing Crosby achieved mainstream dominance with the authoritative performances of Frank Sinatra (the swagger of *Songs for Swingin' Lovers* does indeed seem to imply ownership of the songs). From this peak, it degenerated into the all-purpose crooning of a host of second-rate singers, which only the 'logocentric revolution' of Elvis Presley could displace. The same goes for opera singing between the golden age of Monteverdi and the roulades of Rossini, which Verdi's dramatic declamation rudely interrupted.

The situation now, according to Potter, is pluralistic in the extreme. Crossover, contemporary music and early music all generate their own styles and orthodoxies. Comparing the performances of Montserrat Caballé and Freddie Mercury on their 1980s crossover album *Barcelona* – the former obsessed with technique and beautiful sounds, the latter text-centred and expressive – he perceives 'the limitations of classical singing, and the potential of a form of popular singing to supplant it, given a context which can overcome the ideological circumstances of classical music performance'. Another revolution is on the way. This over-excited analysis is all of a piece with Potter's self-conscious utopianism – he is, after all, founder member of an early-music vocal group, 'Red Byrd', which has the explicit 'aim of addressing questions of class as part of its agenda'. That this engagement with class politics seems largely to involve singing Renaissance music 'in modern regional accents, each singer using a local accent with which he is familiar', speaks for itself.

There is everything to be said for historical accounts of aesthetic phenomena that trade in political, social and ideological explanation. The social status of classical singing as a bourgeois consumable, but with its roots in the liturgical music of an authoritative and universal Church, is indeed a subject worthy of an 'external' history rather than the internal, 'disciplinary' study to which vocal history is usually subject. But the historical thinking Potter brings to bear is too narrowly ideological to achieve a convincing balance between nuance and generalisation (Perry Anderson's synoptic works of the late 1980s and doctrinaire Budapest musicology of the 1970s seem to have played crucial roles in Potter's formation as a historian). For instance, over-concerned to find the roots of classical 'authority' in Church and State power during the Middle Ages, he misses the embarrassment that the theatricality of what he calls 'stylised singing' could create within an ecclesiastical milieu (from St Jerome to the Reformation, Bach's Passions, Verdi's Requiem and beyond).

Potter's basic cyclical theory of singing style is too schematic to fit the evidence (where is Mozart in all this?); and, fixated on the ideological, it comes to ignore the aesthetic and intellectual roots of stylistic change, rather than trying to bind the two together. Throughout the period of the musical 'renaissance', from the Burgundians to Berio, there has been a tension between the formal and the expressive, and between the decorative and the intentional. Questions of vocal style, the often conflicting demands of text delivery and quasi-instrumental sonority and articulation, are an added layer in this wider history. Moreover, definitions of expressivity shift. For instance, in English song of the twentieth century, an insistence on syllabic settings, the doctrine that true expressivity and closeness to the text required one note per syllable, gave way, in Britten's music, to a return to Purcellian melisma, but melisma absolutely rooted in the text. Both approaches are true to their own notions of expressivity (though it's clear which is the greater music: Britten's).

It ought to be an advantage in engaging with the history of singing to be a singer oneself, as Potter is. Yet, as a singer, I find very little in Potter's account of singing that squares with my own experience. He associates what he calls the modern voice, with its typically 'low larynx' technique, with received pronunciation. Yet, it's a commonplace among singing teachers that English RP is anathema to the forward placement central to the sort of singing known as *bel* canto; and I doubt if the notion of RP makes much sense to a German or Italian.

More generally, Potter erects a barrier between classical singing and theatricality (opera aside) which is debilitating. A song recital is as much of a theatrical performance as an opera, albeit with a smaller repertoire of gesture, a smaller stage, and only one prop (the piano) to work with. The body, *pace* Potter, is a vital expressive instrument in concert and recital; and the re-creation of emotion by singers is no more dishonest or 'synthesised' than in any other art-form. Art is always, to some extent, artifice, a fact that has been disturbing analysts since Plato. Personally, at the most emotional parts of a work I tend to be absorbed and focused, somehow inside the music, not outside it making judgement, as Potter seems to think is the norm; it is precisely at moments of weakness, when a technical anxiety takes hold or audience feedback is interrupted, that one stands outside the performance, to its detriment. Emotional focus is the touchstone of the best performances; which is not the same as saying that one shares exactly in the emotional state that one is representing.

Authoritative singing, emotional focus and the song recital as theatre – Dietrich Fischer-Dieskau, the pre-eminent German baritone of the Cold War period, represents all these things. In fact, if one wanted to give credence to the notion of vocal authority, Fischer-Dieskau would be a good place to start. For, at his peak, from the mid-1950s to the mid-70s, Fischer-Dieskau seemed almost to own German art-song, the Lied. This was reflected in a series of magisterial recordings, many of them released as almost scholarly complete editions in imposing box sets; and including eight commercial recordings of the supreme work in the genre, Schubert's *Winterreise*. The Fischer-Dieskau voice – a lyric baritone with an exquisite *mezza* voice and thrilling top – was melded to an engagement with text and an extraordinary platform manner to produce performances the like of which I have never seen, before or since. They made life difficult for other Lieder-singing baritones, near-contemporaries like Hermann Prey, or later generations – 'the next Fischer-Dieskau?' was always the lurking question.

This is not to say that Fischer-Dieskau was not criticised. The so-called, indeed miscalled, 'interventionist' approach to Lieder singing was the critical target, one that Hans

Neunzig's biography (somewhat haltingly rendered into English by Kenneth Whitton) identifies, only to dismiss it with too little thought. There is a tension in Lieder-singing between the demands of text and those of musical line, and every performance represents a compromise between the two. In no way would Fischer-Dieskau have made a reasoned decision to jab at particular words by way of emphasis; when he worked through *Die schöne Müllerin* with me in 1995, his emphasis was, almost to a fault, on singing line and constant vibration of the voice. In that sense, he is very much a singer of the old school, unswayed by the newfangled expressionism of the period-performance movement. There certainly was a change in Fischer-Dieskau's singing between the sheer easy beauty of the EMI recordings of the mid-1950s, and the DG recordings of much the same repertoire in the 1960s and 70s, but age and the demands of a heavy operatic schedule explain a lot. For any singer, if the odd phrase is broken up or the occasional word hammered at, it may often be a momentary conspiracy between imaginative emphasis and sheer frustration that the voice doesn't move in the accustomed way. It's something that in live performance may well work the old magic, but which recording will pinpoint and, in its own way, exaggerate.

Neunzig's book is largely an uncritical account of the great man's life and career, including sixty pages on the ancillary areas into which his insatiable artistic drive has led him – an accomplished painter, a prolific writer, and, of late, a conductor and reciter. It discreetly covers what can only have been the deepest trauma of his life, the death of his wife, the cellist Irmgard Poppen, in childbirth. There is a touching reminder here of the personal closeness that musical partnership can breed – Jörg Demus, one of

Fischer-Dieskau's accompanists, came to live in his Berlin house in the wake of Poppen's death, coaxing his companion back to music.

What of Fischer-Dieskau's authority as a vocalist? Can one provide some sort of analysis beyond the appreciation of his natural and acquired vocal and interpretative strengths? That singular authority extended only as far as the Lied. While he was a successful opera singer, his ventures into jealously guarded foreign territory – Falstaff or Iago, say – were often disputed. His dominance in Lieder sprang from very particular circumstances. He was part of a new generation, forged in tyranny and defeat (his first *Winterreise* was given in a prisoner-of-war camp), and he offered a very different sort of singing to a public, at home and abroad, that wanted to forget Wagnerian grandiloquence. Fischer-Dieskau's soft singing was unique and new. In a concert hall it focused the attention of the audience, drawing them in and holding them still. On record, it offered a sort of intimacy and a return to the domestic roots of song-singing as *Hausmusik*. 'What is this whispering?' the older baritone Gerhard Hüsch is supposed to have complained. The close miking which Fischer-Dieskau demanded throughout his career – even more striking in the mono days – puts one in mind of a Sinatra or Fitzgerald, a new sort of Lieder-singing for a reinvented medium.

Benefiting, personally and professionally, from the *Wirtschaftswunder* – a period after war and ideological storm reminiscent in its domesticity of Schubert's Vienna – Fischer-Dieskau's authority as a Lieder singer was underlined by his role as a cultural ambassador, taking the German language and German music all over the world in the company of his English accompanist, Gerald Moore. He was the first

German singer in Norway after 1945, and the first German musician to make a tour of Israel. There won't be another like him, because of the voice and the intelligence in it and behind it, but also because his working life coincided with a particular historical moment which has gone.

1998

French Baroque Music

The big story in classical music over the past quarter-century – apart from the boom–bust banalities of the CD/Three Tenors/Classic FM era and the after-party headache that the classical industry is now suffering and endlessly bemoaning – has been the variously named 'authentic', 'early music' or 'period instrument' revolution. As far as vocal music is concerned, the movement has been misdiagnosed. It's not really a matter of philosophical debates as to whether and exactly how we follow composers' own conceptions of their works, or recover the precise aesthetic or sound of a long-lost age. Far more important has been the recovery of lost repertoire and the reinvigoration of the familiar.

Handel is the perfect example. The faux-pious stodginess of the Handel performances we can hear on early recordings (*Messiah* usually takes the biscuit) has been replaced by a lightly sprung rhetorical style that makes the music live, and speak to the postmodern ear. At the same time, new works have been uncovered, and have reinforced the reinvention of Handel as entrepreneur, adventurer, man of the theatre and scion of Italy rather than precursor of worthy Victorian Teutonism. The operas and the oratorios can be magnificent theatre, as productions at English National Opera and Glyndebourne have shown, but some of the greatest masterpieces remain too little known – the searing *Tamerlano* with its extraordinary onstage suicide conveyed in impassioned arioso, or *Agrippina*, Handel's take on political and sexual decadence at Nero's court.

Even so, Handel remains relatively easy for the British operatic system to take on board. Handel's operas were written for a London arts world that still exists. It is, and was, a world intermittently suspicious of the aesthetic claims of opera and unable or unwilling to provide a secure financial structure to support its ambitions. Handel's *Samson* was not the only one battling against the Philistine hosts. So it remains a fact that Handel's operas, masterpieces though they clearly are, are also highly revivable because they are highly affordable: small orchestras, small ensembles, relatively modest in spectacle.

Another area of repertoire that has been opened up in this period revolution is the French baroque. But French baroque opera has been revived in France for much the same reasons Handel has triumphed in England: the cultural ecologies of the eighteenth and twenty-first centuries are remarkably similar. French baroque opera – Lully, Charpentier, Rameau – is, with its prologues, ballets and large forces, very expensive to put on. And it is only in a culture where the money for such display is abundant and where the political importance of cultural display is accepted (namely France in either its baroque or postmodern incarnations) that this can happen. We hardly ever see Rameau's operas in England. Next month, that great promoter of French baroque opera, William Christie, brings Rameau's last opera, *Les Boréades* (first ever complete performance given by John Eliot Gardiner, let's remember) from Paris to London. Rameau's *Platée* was staged during the Royal Opera's exile from Covent Garden, but no other recent staging of a French baroque opera springs to mind. Recently Glyndebourne cancelled plans for Rameau's *Hippolyte et Aricie* with Simon Rattle, who had transfixed

Salzburg with *Les Boréades* only a few years previously.

French baroque opera in Britain suffers from a sort of vicious circle of relative neglect. Without the tradition of cultural exceptionalism that kick-started the rediscovery of these works in France, extensively supported by regional government and French business, there are few paths to establishing the repertoire by building the audience. But a production of Charpentier's dazzling *Médée* would certainly be a vehicle for a great mezzo-soprano actress and a revelation for London audiences.

The other problem for French baroque music is the air of specialism that hangs about it. When, say, Simon Rattle conducts the music we can sense it edging into the mainstream. As a singer immersed in the German voice-and-piano tradition that has conquered world concert halls – Schubert, Schumann, Brahms and Wolf – I came to French song through the Romantic and post-Romantic repertory of composers such as Fauré, Debussy, Duparc and Poulenc. These *mélodies* (nineteenth- and early twentieth-century Romantic French songs), powerful and extraordinary as they are, and despite the fame of standards such as Fauré's 'Après un rêve', remain, for various reasons, a specialism. They don't, on the whole, fill concert halls or sell CDs in large numbers. The music itself is subtle and harmonically complex. And the promoters of the music themselves have presented it as a specialism, with an off-putting sense that one has to have 'the style'; something one doesn't really think of when singing Schubert, where a natural expressivity is valued above all.

Studying the French baroque in preparation for a concert that will mix together intimate airs and operatic arias, I realised that this notion of specialism isn't recent, but is built into the warp and weft of French vocal music from the year dot. The idea of *le bon goût*, a sort of hypostasised good taste, was promoted by seventeenth- and eighteenth-century writers on French music. And both foreigners and Frenchmen found French music problematic. Fanny Burney's father Charles, the great historian of music, was tickled by what he saw as French complacency about their musical tradition: 'It is amusing to see how contented mankind has ever been in the most rude and uncultivated ages of the world, with their own talents and accomplishments.' This wasn't just rosbif sneering. Even Voltaire was convinced that 'French music is not pleasing to any other nation' – the prosody peculiar, the melody slow, the instrumental music 'monotonous'.

As I sit down to learn a selection of wonderful French music written between the early seventeenth and mid-eighteenth centuries this seems an extraordinary charge to make. One of the great things about this music, from the simple *airs de cours* produced in the troubled years of the early seventeenth century as a sort of nostalgic comforter, to the grander fare of the age of absolutism, is indeed its specificity, a harmonic language and melodic contour that is just different from its Italian, English or German counterparts. As with French movies, a whole different world opens up.

At the same time, it is remarkable to discover obscure music that can measure up to the greatest. Corneille's poetry from *Le Cid* set by Charpentier is a mini-cycle on honour and despair to match Schubert's essays in alienation. Rameau's cantatas blend French grace with harmonic experiment and emotional intensity, and deserve to be part of the mainstream. Hippolyte's lament from Rameau's first opera

Hippolyte et Aricie is an aria to stand alongside the best of Handel, Mozart or Puccini.

'A good musician', Rameau wrote in 1722, 'ought to surrender himself to all the characters he wishes to depict and, like a skilful actor, put himself in the place of the speaker, imagine himself in the localities where the different events he wishes to represent occur, and take in these the same interest as those most concerned.' This is how French baroque music comes to life; but it also gives a sense of what this music can be for its audience. It is a challenge – but one well worth taking when the treasures to be uncovered are so singular, and so dazzling.

2003

Monteverdi's *Orfeo*

The formative days of opera were charged with an anxiety about the idea of characters suddenly bursting into song (still, perhaps, an issue for the art-form today). Claudio Monteverdi, however, found a rather elegant way to circumvent the problem. He chose Orpheus as the subject for his opera – a musician, whose story was, in part, about music.

Monteverdi's *Orfeo* was very nearly the first opera ever written: premiered in 1607, it was perhaps the third or fourth play entirely set to music. At the time, Monteverdi was employed at the court of the powerful Gonzaga family in Mantua, northern Italy; his *favola in musica*, as he called it, was premiered under the aegis of Francesco Gonzaga and the Accademia Degli Invaghiti, a typical Renaissance society of learned gentlemen.

The story is derived from the version of the Orpheus myth found in Ovid's *Metamorphoses*. Eurydice, the wife of the great singer and musician Orpheus, dies. He, heartbroken, ventures into the Underworld, charming Hades' inhabitants with his skill in song and the lyre to allow him to bring Eurydice back to life. Hades grants his request, but on one condition: as he leaves the Underworld, with her following in his footsteps, he must not look back. But he cannot resist the temptation to do so, and their chance is lost: Eurydice disappears into the Underworld for ever.

Not surprisingly, many other composers based operas on the same myth. But it was Monteverdi, four hundred years ago, who defined the huge debate about opera that remained live for composers such as Wagner and Strauss, and is still crucial today: which comes first, the words or the music?

Orfeo is fascinating in that it has an extremely grown-up, sophisticated libretto, by Monteverdi's colleague at the Gonzaga court, Alessandro Striggio. It is not just tacked on to the music. Although Monteverdi's operas were not performed during the nineteenth century (*Orfeo* had its British concert premiere, for instance, only in 1924), they had been investigated by the English musicologist Charles Burney, and Wagner vaguely knew them. In the German composer's quest to create the complete art-work – *Gesamtkunstwerk* – *Orfeo* would have provided a better exemplar than what he would have regarded as the 'debased' forms of later Italian opera by composers such as Bellini.

I perform a lot of German nineteenth-century song, and I think of *Orfeo* as being the seventeenth-century Italian version of Lieder. It comes back to the way Monteverdi treats the text: the word-setting is incredibly skilful, and he uses the nature and rhythm of the words to dictate how the music is coloured.

In fact, the lead in *Orfeo* is one of the few operatic roles that suits a Lieder singer's approach. Opera nowadays tends to be about big orchestras playing loudly. So, in order for a singer's sound to carry, detail, subtlety and nuance are ironed out. You cannot use the colour you would as a Lieder singer – the colour that an actor might use to read a poem, to infuse the words with coldness, or harshness, or richness. But you can do that with Britten's operas, for instance, and you can do it with the subtle scoring of an opera like *Orfeo*.

There is also an incredible freedom to *Orfeo* that is one of its great attractions. Monteverdi was making up the rules of this new form as he went along. There are extraordinarily beautiful three- and five-part madrigals, wonderful dance music, and (something that is lost in later opera) sophisticated recitatives which take flight with intensity of passionate melodic invention. In preparing a recent Barbican performance of *Orfeo*, we worked on making the recitative sound close to speech. You don't want to lose the metrical sense, but you want it to feel as if the words are coming into your head there and then. There is something jazz-like about the syncopation and freedom of it.

Can an opera written so long ago, first performed under what might seem alien circumstances have currency and power for us today? I believe it can. When operas of this period were being 'rediscovered' in the early twentieth century, they were often regarded as 'primitive', just as much of the visual art of the Renaissance was. But *Orfeo* is nothing of the sort; on the contrary, it is rather knowing and self-referential – even, in its way, postmodern.

The allegorical character Musica, for instance, teases the audience, clearly showing us that what we are engaged in is artifice, not reality. And Orfeo himself is complex. When he first sings of his passion for Eurydice, he is full of self-mockery, teasing himself about the fact that he was so mournful in his pursuit of her love. This makes it all the more horrifying when the news arrives that she is actually dead.

The opera has its comic moments, too. When Orfeo sings to Charon, the oarsman who rows the dead over the Styx to the Underworld, and from whom he must beg a lift, he is supposed to astonish the old man with his brilliance. In fact, Orfeo fails to convince him, and is able to get across the river (rowing himself) only because Charon falls asleep. Orfeo also has a self-centred strain: when he leaves the Underworld with Eurydice in his wake, he sings about his all-powerful lyre, rather than about his love for his beloved. There's a sense that, in losing Eurydice, he is being punished for his self-obsession.

Works such as *Orfeo* are often described as 'mannered', meant as a criticism. But even quite extreme, or alien, conventions – such as those in Kabuki theatre – need not prevent a work from being moving. As a performer, I have to discard what I know about a piece of music and respond to it emotionally and physically. I think that is how we all respond to art, in the end.

2003

Handel at the Opera

Review of Winton Dean, *Handel's Operas, 1726–1741*

Handel's operas are at an all-time high of availability and critical renown. Every month, it seems, brings a new, starry recording, often of a work unheard since the eighteenth century. In our London opera houses, two Handelian masterpieces, *Orlando* (Ariosto co-opted into the service of eighteenth-century politeness) and *Agrippina* (a Venetian satirical prequel to Monteverdi's *L'incoronazione di Poppea*), have recently overlapped their runs and played to full and appreciative audiences. Handel is better off than he was in his own day, when the attempt to run two rival opera companies in London bankrupted the genre and ultimately put an end to one of its golden ages.

In many ways this is the biggest revolution to have happened in the operatic repertoire since the rehabilitation of *Così fan tutte*. For while a lot of baroque music has of course been revived by specialists, Handel has been storming the citadels. In Munich, spiritual home of Strauss and Wagner, with a powerful Mozartian tradition, young and sophisticated audiences have flocked to see 'postmodern' productions of Handel opera, staged by Richard Jones, David Alden and Martin Duncan. And the most conservative bastion of all, New York's Metropolitan Opera, has put on Handel opera as a vehicle not only for a star soprano, Renée Fleming, but also for a star counter-tenor, David Daniels, giving status to a voice previously largely restricted to the Early Music ghetto.

The musicological and critical turnaround has been, perhaps, even more extraordinary – bastardised versions of Handel operas were, after all, playing in German opera houses well before the Early Music movement and the new-wave producers got to them. In 1932, a provocative but essentially misguided Theodor Adorno confidently assumed that such works deserved to be silenced, arguing that:

> according to very specific and reliable technical criteria the musical quality of the overwhelming majority of Handel's works cannot justify their performance nowadays . . . the essential lesson that Handel has to teach is one of economy of means. The best part of this was assimilated into the bare, austere power of Beethoven's oeuvre. All that remains today is the hieratic gesture, which no longer suffices.

This view can have been founded only on the unfamiliarity, indeed unavailability, of great swathes of the composer's work. Surely that characterisation of his music as 'hieratic gesture' is bound up with the Handel inherited from the nineteenth century, the Handel of the overblown *Messiah* denuded of its fleetness of foot and rhetorical cadence, the Handel of the fabulously and appropriately hieratic *Zadok the Priest*. The Handel we know today, that of *Acis and Galatea*, of *Semele*, of *Agrippina*, *Tamerlano* and *Ariodante*, is another composer altogether.

Yet scepticism about the operas continued to hold sway for a long time, even among committed Handelians. In 1959, a scholar thoroughly sympathetic to Handel's dramatic endeavours could nevertheless still write off the operas:

> The total impression made by Handel's operas is one of frustrated genius. However heroic his attempt to transcend the convention, it was – given the circumstances of his period and his character –

bound to end in failure . . . his operas scarcely stand up as fully fashioned works of art.

The scholar in question was Winton Dean, who has devoted his professional life to the study of Handel and whose massive and appreciative study of Handel's operas has just reached completion, with the publication of its second volume, *Handel's Operas, 1726–1741*.

Dean's 1959 dismissal of the operas is found in the prelude to his equally magisterial apologia and study, *Handel's Dramatic Oratorios and Masques*. That book exhaustively established sources and documents for the works in question, while at the same time making the case for the dramatic genius exhibited in a massive and varied body of work stretching from the pastoral serenata (*Acis and Galatea*) via biblical epic (*Saul*) to the final spiritual sublimities and subjectivism of *Theodora* and *Jephtha*. Anything but *Messiah*, essentially.

Rediscovering the genius of Handel meant rescuing him from the sheer success and diffusion of that extraordinary work, along with the music of 'hieratic gesture' and the ersatz Georgian ease of modern arrangements of the *Water Music*. For Dean, in 1959, it meant rescuing Handel from his image as a church composer, and realising that at his best, in the unstaged oratorios as much as in the operas, Handel was a man of the theatre and the inventor (however gropingly) of 'an organic form satisfying the strictest musical and dramatic canons'.

Dean found in the best of Handel's English oratorios the creation of a dramatic art-form that, 'in its spiritual themes, its treatment of the chorus, and its combination of elements from music, drama, ritual, spectacle, and dance . . . suggested a striking parallel with the tragedy of the Greeks'. Handel produced something that the Florentines and their successors, who invented the idea of opera in the late sixteenth century, had dreamed of, but which few of their followers convincingly achieved. The great irony, of course, was that the unstaged oratorios were now being viewed as successful in a way that the staged operas were not, hamstrung as they seemed to be by the conventions of *opera seria* – the *da capo* aria, the paucity of ensemble, the enervating reams of *secco* recitative and, all in all, the lack of what Dean called 'structural rhythm'.

Dean's subsequent books on Handel – his lectures on *opera seria* and the two-volume study of the operas – have been a sort of penance paid for this anathema. He has come to embrace Handel as the missing link between Monteverdi and Mozart, a worthy companion of Verdi and Wagner; the composer of forty or so successful operas, among them at least half-a-dozen exemplary masterpieces (*Tamerlano*, *Giulio Cesare*, *Rodelinda*, *Ariodante*, *Alcina* and *Orlando*) which can stand worthily alongside *Poppea*, *Figaro*, *Otello*, or *Tristan*.

Dean's volte-face is not really surprising. As he notes in an epilogue to *Handel's Operas, 1726–1741*, 'it presently dawned on me that the mighty dramatist of the oratorios was unlikely to have sprung from nowhere'. His work on the operas is a monument of dedicated scholarship, an indispensable resource for anyone writing about or staging Handel's operatic works. He gives us all the information there is to be had about the occasion of a work, the source of its libretto and previous settings of it, the singers, the stage directions (including Handel's own manuscript notations on staging), the source materials and versions, the stage history. To have all this in one work is remarkable. The historical introductions to each group of operas are admirably clear.

The rivalry between the two great divas Faustina Bordoni and Francesca Cuzzoni is given due weight – one contemporary report talks of 'an unhappy Breach being made betwixt them since their first Reconcilement, occasioned by one of them making Mouths at the other while she was singing'. So is the exhausting conflict between Handel's operatic endeavours and those undertaken by the so-called Opera of the Nobility. These fed off divisions in the Royal Family and led to the temporary breakdown of the composer's health, in 1737, and ultimately, no doubt, to his gradual migration away from opera into the more profitable field of the oratorio.

Dean's discovery in his painstaking pilgrimage through the entire corpus of Handel's extant operas has been that there is more variety and more organic thought at work than the generalised view of Handel as *opera seria* composer has allowed for. Handel opera is not a tiresome succession of unrelated *da capo* arias broken up by interminable *secco* recitative. There is structural rhythm and plenty of it. Take *Ariodante*, for example. The *da capo* aria remains the foundation of the work, but it is leavened with shortened aria forms, with six cavatinas, four duets and four sinfonias which set the scene or form part of the action itself. Dean is acute in his discernment both of the dramatic use of tonality (switches in key used to theatrical effect) and of a 'definite tonal plan' based on G minor/major and spanning the whole opera from the overture through to the final chorus.

In one of the epilogues to this volume, Dean considers why Handel's dramatic genius in the operas was for so long hidden. Shrewdly, he identifies pacing as a crucial issue. Theatrical practice in the early eighteenth century embraced and necessitated dramatic continuity. Handel's operas carried on without interruption through the often magnificent scene changes which happened in full view of the audience. This continuity is enhanced by flexibly paced, half-spoken recitatives (the 'sinews' of the opera, as Dean puts it), telescoped cadences and a recognition that the scene, not the aria, is the dramatic unit. Dean sees this as part of the design, regardless of the fact that applause must have impeded dramatic impulse; and this, of course, is a problem with much later opera too (how often are Puccini's arias quite clearly part of the dramatic flow yet reliably capped with raucous applause?).

More questionably, Dean attacks those who use Handel's works 'as the basis of a modern entertainment regardless of their period associations'. He dislikes director-driven opera in the big international opera houses and seems to argue that theatrical values would benefit from a touch of period practice, just as musical values have. The paradox is that the sorts of productions Dean seems to dislike (though he's mostly unspecific), and which have had enormous success in London, Munich and elsewhere, bringing new audiences to appreciate Handel's dramatic genius, have been closely allied with the new musical praxis. The best of them are brilliantly paced and aided in that by the lightening of texture and revival of the notion of rhetorical gesture in baroque music, which the period-instrument revolution has brought. In that sense, these productions are true to something in the spirit of the music which a literal-minded return to eighteenth-century practice or, even more permissively, to something the composer 'would have recognised' (Dean's own phrase), misses.

Dean's aim has been to rehabilitate Handel's operas by assimilating them to the mainstream tradition. He presents Handel as a psychological dramatist and precursor to Mozart and Verdi. Here he seems to be working with a model of characterisation and identity that post-dates the composer, a model that culminates theatrically in the Stanislavskian notion of building a role, and has the psychological realism of the nineteenth-century novel as its touchstone. The golden rule for opera is thus set by the best of the Romantic Age, originating in Vienna with Wolfgang Amadeus Mozart and made problematic, also in Vienna, by the singularly unmusical Sigmund Freud.

But the so-called 'postmodern' directors are, I think, particularly successful in Handel because they have picked up on something genuinely eighteenth century – what the historian Dror Wahrmann has called the *ancien regime* of identity' – in which 'character' was seen as less continuous, more subject to sudden change; in which identity was not bound up with a deep model of psychological particularism. We see this in much eighteenth-century portraiture; and we no longer expect to find the birth of modern realism in the eighteenth-century novel. The art that reflected this understanding dealt very much in types rather than unique individuals; and a porous notion of identity was part of its currency. Neither interiority nor individuality were at a premium. We would not expect to find Mozart's Countess or Verdi's Iago (how different from Shakespeare's . . .) in a Handelian opera.

This approach dovetails nicely with the view of the philosopher Peter Kivy that the *da capo* aria is perfectly suited to the dominant early eighteenth-century theory of the passions, inherited from Descartes: hence the obsessive return to the same emotions in the *da capo*, and the violent changes of affect between arias. By the standards that have obtained since the birth of sentimentalism and which govern our expectations of hitherto mainstream opera, these are not normal people but a bunch of what Kivy calls 'emotional fanatics'. In one sense, then, Handel's operas are indeed, as Winton Dean said all those years ago, barely 'fully fashioned works of art'. It has taken the late twentieth century, with its aesthetic of fragmentation, to do justice to a dramatic art in which much of the musical material is transferable between characters or borrowed from utterly different scenarios; in which personality is akin to costume, as characters act out clichés or new-minted ideas inside a structure that values juxtaposition and contrast more than logical and consistent development.

How appropriate that Handel himself seems such a Protean individual, a shape-changer who cut a figure among French Calvinists, Roman Cardinals and the Georgian aristocracy alike. He started his life in Halle as Georg Friedrich Händel and ended it in London as the curiously hybrid George Frideric Handel. He boldly and extensively appropriated the music of his composer contemporaries as his own. In his own lifetime, Roubiliac's statue of him as a relaxed eighteenth-century Orpheus was to be seen in Vauxhall Pleasure Gardens; at his death a monument by the same artist was erected in Westminster Abbey. He was a national icon and in many ways a symbol of, or an analogy for, a political system in which a German Lutheran could paradoxically embody the patriotic imperatives of an English aristocratic order. Handel's role within the genesis and bedding-in of the Hanoverian regime – from espionage during Queen Anne's illness to the ideological substance, religious and political, of the oratorios – deserves more attention, as does the political meaning of the operas: not so much in terms of their subject-matter, which only occasionally touches directly on political concerns, as in the way in which they became a focus of political faction (when the King and the Prince of Wales fell out, for instance) or a metaphor for political controversy in pamphlets and wider political discourse (during the Excise Crisis). This is part of a wider European story of the political uses of opera in the *ancien regime* which is beginning to be told, and it locates London very firmly in the European orbit. It would be well worth understanding why, for a period of about thirty years, opera sung in Italian was the focus of such sustained attention by the newly British elites.

2007

My Problem with Mozart

All over the world, opera houses, concert halls and professional and amateur musicians are celebrating Mozart: this month marks two hundred and fifty years since his birth. Particularly ambitious is the Salzburg Festival's plan to perform every one of his operas over a single summer season. As a classical singer I am, inevitably, making my own modest contribution to the celebrations: singing Mozart arias in a recital in Hamburg, and appearing in a production of *Don Giovanni* at the Vienna State Opera. I don't perform a great deal of opera but, having the sort of tenor voice that suits Mozart rather than Verdi, the former looms large in my career as a theatrical performer.

But there is a problem with Mozart, one I readdress every time I sing in one of his operas. It has been said – often – that Mozart tenor roles are boring.

This is an opinion that I am anxious, for obvious reasons, to rebut. The evidence to support it is, however, easy to find. When do people get bored in *The Marriage of Figaro*, otherwise one of the most miraculously satisfying works in the Western canon? When the irritating, and superbly funny, minor character Basilio, a small-town Machiavelli of a singing teacher, insists on singing his aria in the final act, delaying the denouement and spoiling the fun. He is (unfortunately for me) a tenor. The aria is, more often than not, cut.

It's the same but different in *Die Entführung aus dem Serail*, the opera Mozart wrote immediately before *Figaro*. Belmonte, the tenor hero, has a wealth of gorgeous music lavished on him. His three beautiful arias are, however, one, perhaps two, too many for the dramatic structure. 'Wenn der Freude Tränen fließen' and 'Ich baue ganz' interrupt the action and are dramatically inert. While technically challenging, their difficulties are meant to be hidden by the accomplished singer, so that people will notice only if they are sung badly. They do not embody struggle in the way Constanze's bravura aria 'Martern aller Arten' does; many aficionados will come to the opera just to hear the dramatic intensity offered by Constanze's vocal martyrdom. The tension and psychological realism of Belmonte's famous first aria, 'O, wie ängstlich', the ardour of the reunion quartet, the painful rapture of the Belmonte–Constanze duet as they confront death towards the end of the opera – these are, for me, the moments of Belmonte's that live most intensely, both when singing and when listening to the piece. It takes resolute cutting and cunning direction to rescue Belmonte from being a tiresome goody-goody or a self-satisfied prig.

But it's Don Ottavio in *Don Giovanni* who is the most revealing example of my problem with Mozart. Critics and audiences alike complain of his passivity. He stands as the virtuous and ineffective opposition to Giovanni's demonic life force, and is bound to suffer in comparison. But in fact, Act I makes sense for Ottavio in terms of storytelling and dramatic pace. His duet with Donna Anna after her father's murder by Giovanni is powerful and affecting; the aria 'Dalla sua pace' is a touching and economical moment of stasis, theatrically highly effective.

It is the second-act aria, 'Il mio tesoro' – a piece of exquisite time-wasting – that can do for Don Ottavio. This is an aria that explicitly admits it is holding up the action.

'Meanwhile, go and console my beloved,' Ottavio sings as he prepares to alert the authorities to Giovanni's miscreancy. It sounds like a beautiful and irrelevant serenade, and it has had, rather revealingly, a healthy life as a concert aria without dramatic context.

In fact, Mozart only ever intended Ottavio to have one aria. 'Il mio tesoro' was written for the original Prague production, 'Dalla sua pace' as part of the revision for a subsequent run in Vienna. This is often presented as a matter of horses for courses – different sorts of aria for different singers. But it was also, evidently, a case of second thoughts being better than first. Without 'Il mio tesoro', Ottavio rather disappears in Act II, but that is in the nature of the plot, which focuses at that stage on Don Giovanni's supernatural comeuppance.

It's no use worrying that Don Ottavio in his delayed vengeance isn't fleshed out into a operatic Hamlet surrogate. Act I's drama and tenderness and the extraordinary ensembles in both acts should be enough for any tenor. The problem is that many contemporary productions, anxious to placate an underused singer or maximise the use of an expensive tenor, encourage the singer to do both arias. Being one of the tenors all too eager to be placated – if I'm offered a lovely aria to sing, who am I to refuse? – I can't really complain. More beautiful music, less effective drama: it's a commonplace operatic dilemma.

Don Ottavio's inadequacies have been explained as those of an *opera seria* character inhabiting a *dramma giocoso* – a character from the old form inhabiting the new. Yet it strikes me that of all the Mozart roles I have sung, the most satisfying is the title role in a so-called *opera seria*: *Idomeneo*, the earliest opera of Mozart's to be part of the repertoire.

Idomeneo's arias always seem to emerge from the drama, to amplify and intensify it, aided by the brilliant accompanied recitatives that precede them and weave them into the musical-dramatic structure.

Eighteenth-century operas on heroic subjects, mythical or classical, are sometimes seen as the antithesis of Romanticism in music, bound as they are by the rules of classical drama, formal and restrained. This is certainly the world Don Ottavio comes from. Sitting in Milan's La Scala last month, however, listening to Daniel Harding's debut conducting *Idomeneo*, I was struck, despite the anti-Romanticism of Harding's approach in terms of sonority and texture, by the utter Romanticism of the piece. The great, passionate, intense sweep of music that is the first act, from the overture to Idamante's recognition of his long-lost but forbidding father, is Romantic in conception and, like the plays of Shelley or Byron, impossible to represent adequately on stage. It is shattering music of the mind, psychological and intense.

In a peculiar sense, despite the ritual and ceremony of this grand *opera seria*, it's much nearer the inner dramatic world of Schubert or Schumann. For all the beauties of Mozart's more mature stage works – and *Don Giovanni* remains an extraordinary piece of music theatre in which to participate, even if you're playing its least interesting character – *Idomeneo* remains the most satisfying to perform for a tenor, from a selfish point of view at least. It was Mozart's favourite among his operas, too, no doubt as much for what it tries to do as for what it actually achieves.

2006

*This piece made at least one person very annoyed. I was told,
shortly after it appeared, that at a Friends' evening or some such
at Covent Garden, the opera director David McVicar had, to
put it mildly, distanced himself from the piece. The following
day, this appeared in the* Independent:

'Ian Bostridge – and I really want this quoted – goes on about
how Mozart never wrote any interesting roles for the tenor voice,'
McVicar fumes. 'To which my answer is: if you could sing any of
those roles, maybe I would listen to your opinion! I was incandes-
cent with rage. If he could sing Ferrando in *Così* and finds it unre-
warding, I would listen to what he has to say, but since he can't . . .
D'you know what I mean?'

The German Song

Review of Edward F. Kravitt, *The Lied: Mirror of Late Romanticism* and Susan Youens, *Schubert's Poets and the Making of Lieder*

Song has always been at the centre of German culture. More than has been the case in any other European nation, even Italy, song has been an index of nationhood. From the birth of *echt* German nationalism in the early decades of the nineteenth century to the rebirth of a democratic German state in the 1950s, the Lied has been a national totem. Wagner's *Die Meistersinger von Nürnberg* is the most notorious example of song as ideology, but examples abound. A glossy history painting in the Nationalgalerie in Berlin shows muddy Prussians crowded into a fussy Parisian drawing room in 1871; one plays the piano while the others sing. Wholesome German song vanquishes French effeteness. A German movie of the 1940s has the young Elisabeth Schwarzkopf singing Schumann's 'Mondnacht' as the bombs fall. Defeat transformed the picture, but song remained a cultural weapon.

Schwarzkopf saw Lieder-singing after the war as a way of rehabilitating the German language on the world stage. Germans have seen the Lied as a vehicle for distinctly German values. Yet the genius poured into the great tradition of Lieder has transformed what ought to have been a parochial genre into one of the major strands in Romantic music from Beethoven to Richard Strauss.

Despite the cautions of the purists, singers believe that Lieder are not a specialised German export; they belong to everyone. In the work of Schubert, with songs such as 'The Trout' and 'Erl-King', German song is culturally transcendent. If the Lied is less valued today than it has been in the past, this is as much the case in Germany as elsewhere. In London, the Wigmore Hall has a thriving and innovative programme of song recitals rooted in German song; Berlin's Lieder plans for the 1997 Schubert bicentenary are pretty well non-existent.

In *The Lied: Mirror of Late Romanticism*, Edward F. Kravitt reminds us quite how omnipresent a musical genre German song was for fin-de-siècle Germans – twenty Lieder recitals in Berlin in a week, he suggests. The Lied had moved from small-scale private or domestic performance, as *Hausmusik*, to the concert stage when, in the 1850s, Julius Stockhausen started giving public performances of the great centrepieces of the genre, such as Schubert's *Die schöne Müllerin* and Schumann's *Dichterliebe*. It was after 1870 that this modest development blossomed, so that Hugo Wolf, the greatest Lieder composer of the late Romantic period and a famous Viennese figure of the time, could speak of an 'epidemic' of *Liederabende*. More than that, Lieder were performed at fashionable soirées, grand hotels, cabarets, vocal academies and choral societies.

It was in the late nineteenth and early twentieth centuries that the conventions of the song recital were first devised. Today, recitalists range broadly, or so it seems, from the chatty camaraderie of the Americans to the austere aesthetic of the Fischer-Dieskau school. But the theatrical possibilities around 1900 were even wider, though mixed programmes – instrumental and vocal in the same concert – were on the whole abandoned in favour of the solo performer. Coloured lights were suggested as mood-enhancers, and there were wafting scents – heliotrope for love songs, incense for serious outpourings. The pianist was often concealed and green-lit palms recommended as a screen for singers whose gesticulation might detract from their performance. On the other hand, a singer might adopt the garb of a Bacchic reveller, or the white robe of a priest of Apollo.

Alongside these aesthetic excesses, redolent more of Wilde and Beardsley than stern Teutonism, song was a focus of pan-national sentiment, both in recently united Germany, and in painfully excluded Austria. That painted scene of Prussians in 1870s Paris had its real-life echo in the 1890s. During a performance of Wolf's 'Heimweh' (Homesickness) at the Vienna Wagner Verein, the composer was unable to finish a performance of the song, because its sentiments had become the occasion for a noisy demonstration of pan-Germanism.

The nationalist resonances of the Lied had been there from the birth of the modern genre. Schubert failed in his ambitions as an opera composer, partly at least as a result of linguistic chauvinism and the musical dominance of Italians; meanwhile, he wrote songs and song-cycles which declared the musical genius of the German tongue. In the later Romantic period, paradoxes emerged. The Kaiser denounced modern song as too complex and insufficiently rooted in the *Volk*. Yet those composers, such as Mahler, who most famously adopted folk elements into their Lieder, remained sophisticated artists at heart, in the vanguard of contemporary music.

Nevertheless, it is Kravitt's central contention that the late Romantic Lied was essentially a conservative genre.

The composers on whose pre-First World War work he concentrates – Wolf, Mahler, Strauss, Pfitzner and Reger – may have been pushing tonality to its limits, writing what one contemporary called 'sheer harmonic nonsense'; but they remained rooted in the Lied traditions of the 1840s, exemplified by Schumann, which Kravitt brilliantly summarises: the paralleling of tension and release in the poetry with tonal dissonance and consonance; the correlation of changes of place and situation in the poem with modulation in the music; the echoing of the movement to climax in poetry with functional harmonic progression to musical climax; and the underscoring of key words with dissonant chords.

The work that did finally break with tonality – *Das Buch der hängenden Gärten* by Arnold Schoenberg – was a song-cycle, and while it was written six years before the outbreak of war, its consequences were not fully felt until the decade after.

That the dislocations of war were responsible for the triumph of musical avant-gardism, as Kravitt maintains, is less certain. On the one hand, the logic of what is, after all, a very technical discipline pointed firmly in the direction of a tonal crisis well before 1914, whatever the conservative intent of its practitioners. On the other, Schoenbergian modernism was entrenched as an orthodoxy in the West only after the Second World War. Between the wars, a Babel of competing musical tongues ranged from neo-classicism to atonalism to old-fashioned conservative Romanticism. The Lied continued to inspire distinguished work – Richard Strauss, Othmar Schoeck – but the great tradition had evaporated. It was no longer at the cutting edge of musical innovation; and the gramophone was already beginning to undermine the culture of *Hausmusik* on which it had always been founded.

Kravitt's book offers many fresh perspectives, from the influence of histrionic poetry recitation on Wolf's compositional style, to the fashion for overwrought emotion on the concert platform. His discussions of particular composers are acute, particularly in the case of the one real master of song he deals with, Hugo Wolf. It is good to be reminded of the sheer variety in Wolf's songs, from melodically etiolated declamation to the catchiest of tunes. Wolf's potential for popular appeal is something performers have so far failed to get across; he remains a difficult project for the marketing gurus of the recording industry.

With Schubert, by contrast, record companies have had the composer's mythical *Gemütlichkeit* and 'Lilac Time' image to draw on. It is this cosiness that the new Schubert scholarship is trying to dispel, which is all to the good. We now know much more about social conditions in Biedermeier Vienna, and about the political, philosophical, moral and aesthetic preoccupations of Schubert's circle. The only pity has been the amount of ink spilled on the issue of Schubert's sexuality, occasioned by Maynard Solomon's partial readings of a few shards of ambiguous evidence to suggest that the composer was homosexual. The fact is that we know very little about Schubert's sex life, beyond his undoubted contraction of syphilis in the 1820s, and it is a pity to find Susan Youens in her new book, *Schubert's Poets and the Making of Lieder*, adding to the confusion in her tendentious discussion of Schubert's friend, Mayrhofer.

Youens's book contains useful studies of four poets whom Schubert chose to set. They lend depth to our understanding of the literary culture in which Schubert lived, bringing back to life poets who would otherwise remain faceless: Gabriele von Baumberg, the 'Sappho of Vienna'; Theodor Körner, militant German patriot and martyr; the amatory obsessive, Ernst Schulze; and Schubert's one-time roommate, the tortured Imperial censor, Johann Mayrhofer. Each of the four chapters is divided in two. The lives of the poets are followed by discussions of a selection of Schubert's settings of each. The detailed musicological analysis is the least interesting feature of the book, as was the case with Youens's previous studies of *Winterreise* and *Die schöne Müllerin*. In fact, these are not so much analyses as descriptions overlaid with some prosaic word-painting: music set to words to replace words set to music. When you have read Charles Rosen's pyrotechnic accounts of the postlude to Schumann's *Frauenliebe und -leben* or the mixing of memory and desire in Schubert's 'Der Lindenbaum' (both in his recent *The Romantic Generation*), it is difficult to be satisfied with anything less brilliant.

Both Baumberg and Schulze are relatively minor figures in Schubert's output (six and ten songs respectively). Youens can find little in Baumberg's struggles, caught between poetry, a selfish husband and the politics of Bonapartism, to illuminate Schubert's life or work, save the common assertion of an artistic calling in the face of either paternal or paternalistic opposition. Körner was famous above all as the hero of the War of Liberation. His warlike poems were set by many other composers, such as Weber, Friedrich Heinrich Himmel and Friedrich Wilhelm Grund, and his popularity was an index of intense German national feeling during and after the expulsion of Bonaparte. Youens's account of Körner's status as heroic icon, the subject of paintings, odes, cantatas and statuary, does serve to place

Schubert (who met the poet) within a context of post-Napoleonic Europe; but can such a context help to unravel what is central to him as a musician? Schubert's most committed Körner settings are not war poems, but fluent lyrics which, as John Reed has suggested, mark a new development in Schubert's 1815 style. The most extraordinary song dates from a few years after the epoch of war and peace, 'Auf der Riesenkoppe' – a tonally adventurous landscape and hymn of praise looking forward to the style of *Die schöne Müllerin*.

Schubert's work does seem initially to resist being placed within a political or social history, founded as it is in a private world in which love and death are the obsessive material of art. Contextualisation remains, nevertheless, a vital area for further work in studies of Schubert. Withdrawal into the self and alienation from society might be seen as socio-political consequences of the reactionary and oppressive atmosphere of post-Napoleonic Vienna, making that elusive link between the political and the personal; more generally, a mood of repressed liberal nationalism in Vienna may have expressed itself in Schubert's huge ambitions for a distinctly German musical genre.

That sense of oppression blighted the life of Johann Mayrhofer, whose career as a censor, ending in suicide, embodied a conflict between liberal principles privately held and an Austrian reaction rigidly enforced. Mayrhofer is the most important figure in Youens's book, both for his influence on Schubert, and as a poet in his own right. Schubert wrote forty-seven songs on texts by his friend, and they are among the greatest of his middle period. The insinuation of a sexual relationship or affinity, or even of Mayrhofer's own homosexuality (mainly based on unconvincing readings of poems Schubert did not choose to set) is beside the point, really. What drew great music from Schubert was Mayrhofer's mythic idealism (in songs such as 'Frei-williges Versinken') and his persistent melancholia, which suffuses the landscapes of 'Erlafsee' or 'Auf der Donau'. After *Die schöne Müllerin*, and his contraction of syphilis, Schubert, in many of his songs, was to move beyond this, into a poetic realm of isolation and obsession.

Ernst Schulze was one of the poets of this late period, the chronicler of doomed love. Youens skilfully dissects the psychopathology of what she calls his erotomania, expressed in successive obsessions for two sisters, one of whom died prematurely, and distilled into his *Poetisches Tagebuch* of 1822, selections from which Schubert set in the years 1825 and 1826. Youens's work on Schulze has already had one beneficial practical effect, in Graham Johnson's construction and recording for Hyperion of a Schulze–Schubert cycle. These songs were in some sense 'studies' for *Winterreise*, all the differences in form and tonality notwithstanding; most importantly, as Youens puts it, because they involve 'the musical mapping of near-insanity'.

Song composers in the late Romantic period, as Kravitt shows in his book, were straining at the limits of tonality and of expressivity. This tendency was built into the Lied from the outset, with Schubert's tonal freedom and Schumann's tonal instability. In its alliance with the poetry of extremes, the Lied drew on a reservoir of madness. This was partly a question of the Romantic infatuation with the irrational; but was it a coincidence that the three greatest composers of Lieder – Schubert, Schumann and Wolf – all lived in fear of clinical insanity? When the final breakdown of tonality came, the possibilities of teetering on the edge were gone. The dissolution of tonality meant the disappearance of the Romantic language of irrationality and the end of a century of pre-eminence for the pianoforte Lied.

1996

For the Schubert Bicentenary

Review of Christopher H. Gibbs (ed.), *The Cambridge Companion to Schubert*; Elizabeth Norman McKay, *Franz Schubert*; and Susan Youens, *Schubert, Müller and 'Die schöne Mullerin'*

Franz Schubert's music was recognised as radical in his own time. 'Anxious striving after originality and continual modulation,' complained one Leipzig critic in 1820. A more sympathetic Dresden notice from 1825 pointed to a unique alliance of intense feeling and musical theory, calling Schubert, significantly, a 'musical painter'.

A song such as 'Gretchen am Spinnrade' does indeed paint a sound-picture, a detailed and specific picture of a spinning wheel at work (as Charles Rosen points out in the new *Cambridge Companion to Schubert*), using it to depict the flux of sensibility within Gretchen herself. The wheel spins, spins faster, stops and restarts as her mood shifts. Realistic detail used to expressive effect: this is something Schubert returned to throughout his career as a song composer.

Schubert spent surprisingly little time with other musicians, at least until the very end of his life. Many of his friends were writers, but several others were, significantly for this 'musical painter', visual artists – including his own brother Karl, Josef Teltscher, Leopold Kupelwieser and, most famously, the arch-Romantic Moritz von Schwind. Given how few documents we have relating to Schubert's life (little of consequence has been uncovered since Otto Erich Deutsch's collection of documentary materials was published in 1946, as the footnotes to Elizabeth Norman McKay's new biography demonstrate), visual images exist in relative abundance, drawn and painted by his friends. They have a profound impact on our conception of Schubert's character and of his world.

First among them in iconic power is Schwind's *Ein Schubert-Abend bei Joseph von Spaun*, a picture that has transmitted that special notion of a concert for and among friends, a 'Schubertiade', into the historical imagination. The humble, bespectacled composer sits at the keyboard, somewhat eclipsed by his expansive singing colleague, Johann Michael Vogl, whose gesturing hand is almost peremptory. In the audience, rapt with attention, sit men and women, artists and amateurs, of more or less eminence – Grillparzer, Spaun, Schönstein, among others. These are Schubert's friends and patrons, presided over by a portrait of the 'muse' of his later years, the Countess Caroline von Esterházy ('Everything is dedicated to you,' Schubert had told her, according to Schönstein). Only Schubert's closest friend in his later years, the rakish Franz von Schober, appears unaffected by the music, as he flirts with his fiancée. Schwind's sepia drawing, dated 1868, was a historical fiction, a composite and a retrospective idealisation: 'an old gentleman', as he wrote, 'chattering about events at which he was present in his youth and to which he still remains attached in his heart'. It is this vision of Schubert and his circle, cosy and domestic, that, pushed to its extreme, informed the early twentieth-century sentimental myth of stage and screen, Schubert the tubby tunesmith with his clutch of charming friends, lovelorn but creative. Nevertheless, there is undoubtedly a truth buried in the myth, a Biedermeier compound of bourgeois sentimentality and individualism, situated in a political context where the best response to the failure of revolutionary ideas and the insidious presence of Prince Metternich's reaction seemed to be surrender to the outside world (many of Schubert's friends were state functionaries), withdrawal into the self and the cultivation of intense personal relationships.

Two watercolours by Leopold Kupelwieser, painted in Schubert's lifetime, extend the vision of affectionate domesticity. In the first, Schubert and Kupelwieser himself saunter behind their friends, a dozen or so men and women indecorously squeezing into a single carriage, 'for a joke', in Schober's words. In the second Schubert sits at a piano in the foreground, a dog at his feet, left hand on the keyboard, rather solemnly observing a game of charades. The word being acted out is 'Rheinfall', the Rhine Falls. Schober tells us that the ladies and gentlemen had already presented the first syllable 'complacently assuring each other that they were clean' ('rein'). Now, in the picture, they are depicting the Fall, taking the parts of Adam, Eve, the tree, the serpent, God, and the angel with his flaming sword. It was the dissolute Schober who commissioned the picture, and in it he takes the part of the tempter.

There is something too arch to be accidental, both in Schober's role-playing, and in that punning juxtaposition of purity and sinning. Schubert's friends were well aware of the dangers Schober represented for the composer. Bauernfeld satirised the poet as a charming but pretentious good-for-nothing – Pantaloon – in a sketch read at Schober's house at New Year in 1826. Pierrot (Schubert) and Harlequin (Schwind) loll and smoke under Pantaloon's malign influence. 'I see the true significance of life in repose,' he declares. It is a long way from this to the 'slough of moral degradation' into which Schober led Schubert, leaving him, according to Josef Kenner, 'bathed in slime'. The irony is that it was Schubert's carousing and contraction of syphilis, under Schober's influence, that acted as an intensifier and a release from relative idleness, triggering the flood of works in the last five years of his life that makes him one of the most prolific composers of all time. 'What I produce', the composer wrote in 1824, 'is due to my understanding of music and to my sorrows.'

Elizabeth Norman McKay's biography of the composer is the fullest account yet of the dualities in Schubert's life, embodied by Schober on the one hand and, on the other, Schubert's old school-friend, the loyal and long-suffering Josef von Spaun. Drawing on the work of David Gramit, McKay makes a convincing case for the importance of what she calls the 'Bildung circle', a group of Schubert's friends devoted with high idealism to the 'love of all that is good'. Spaun was central to the group, as was Johann Mayrhofer, the poet of almost fifty of Schubert's songs, and his flatmate for two years. The group and its yearbook *Beiträge zur Bildung für Jünglinge* (Contributions towards the Education of Young Men) are the serious subtext to the whole idea of a Schubert circle immersed in friendship and political withdrawal (all the more ironic that it was reported to the political police as a suspicious organisation). The ideal world was held to exist in and through art, and aesthetic issues were earnestly researched and debated. This was not only a support group tailor-made for a young and ambitious composer (pushing suitable texts in his direction, forwarding plans for publication), but an ideological motor. Spaun's aesthetic theorising, unusually, placed music at the forefront of the arts, direct and powerful in its effects; and the Bildung preference for classical restraint over Romantic longing clearly affected Schubert's projects and tastes in these early years up to 1820. He was certainly not idle in these years, producing around three hundred and sixty of his thousand opus numbers in the period November 1814 to September 1816.

Yet the works that define the orbit of Schubert's genius – *Winterreise*, the later piano sonatas, the string quintet, the D minor and G major quartets, the 'Unfinished' and 'Great' C major symphonies – were produced in the latter years, after Schober's dissipations had both interrupted the flow of Schubert's work, and diverted it into new channels suffused with Romantic struggles and premonitions of death. One of the special qualities of Schubert's mature style is surely its eerie juxtaposition of the domestic and the savage, the dance interrupted by the angry outburst, the arrogant coexisting with the cosy (think of the way the middle section of 'Rückblick' insinuates itself into the angry flight of the bulk of the song). Despite all the caveats about the impertinence of biographical criticism, it is difficult to avoid attributing that quality to the way in which the respectable and the seedy, the elated and the depressed, the idealistic and the cynical interacted in Schubert's life.

In his essay in the *Cambridge Companion to Schubert*, the editor, Christopher Gibbs, remarks on the way in which succeeding generations have appropriated the composer, constructing their own image of him, just as the first generation of family and friends referred, affectionately but possessively, to 'our Schubert'. Issues of sexuality or gender have been there from the outset. Schumann's contrast between a 'masculine' Beethoven and a 'feminine' Schubert was made specifically in the context of the 'symphonic' writing of the 'Grand Duo'. Later in the century, when the bodies of the two composers were exhumed, the critical metaphor was reified in the most extraordinary way: 'It was extremely interesting physiologically', wrote an observer, 'to compare the compact thickness of Beethoven's skull and the fine, almost feminine thinness of Schubert's.' A biographer two years later referred to the 'almost womanly organisation' of Schubert's skull. It was as if, in the absence of women composers who might be admitted to the pantheon, a male composer was required to represent female identity through his music.

Recent writing about Schubert has become frustratingly focused on the issue of what Maynard Solomon calls his 'primary sexual orientation'. There is no suggestion in Solomon's work that this need have had any direct impact on his music, in the essentialist idiom of the nineteenth-century critics; but Schubert's supposed adoption of an alienated homosexual identity in a morally repressive Viennese regime has been seen as a key to the nature of his social life. The first problem is that evidence one way or the other is so slight, the critical debate larded with tendentious misreadings (particularly on Solomon's part, though that does not damn his entire case). There is plenty of evidence of Schubert's interest in women; most of it in later memoirs (which raises reasonable suspicions about reliability), but some in the rawer form of diaries and letters. Solomon's own thesis is based on the notion that a quotation from Benvenuto Cellini in Bauernfeld's diary ('Schubert is out of sorts; he needs "young peacocks"') might point to an appetite for young men. It might, it might not; and references to peacocks might refer only, as McKay cautiously suggests, to 'pleasure and conviviality' in a general rather than a specific sense.

Sexuality in the Schubert circle is difficult to interpret.

The Platonic tone and structure of the Bildung circle (young men led to virtue by their seniors) went hand in hand with intensely romantic personal relationships. That these could be mediated through music is something David Gramit points out in an essay in the *Cambridge Companion*, citing an 1816 letter from the key Bildung figure, Anton Ottenwalt, aged twenty-six, to the errant fringe player, Franz von Schober, aged nineteen:

The tones carried me away . . . I . . . gave friend Karl my right hand and put my left around our beloved Ferdinand, who sat arm in arm with Kenner. He drew me closer with his right arm, and as the tones thus spoke directly into the soul, I felt the gentle, fervent press of their hands, and I had to look back and forth into their faces and their beloved eyes, they sat so still, pleasantly moved by the music . . . and I gazed at them so, thinking: oh, you good souls, you are indeed happy in your innocence. Music makes you gentler, but not sad, not upset; what your heart desires you grasp in the hand of a friend, and you know no other wishes, you whom the melody gives only loftier waves.

It is the cultural context of this sort of intense male friendship that needs to be understood if we are to unpick the dynamic of the Schubert circle. In the context of Biedermeier reaction, and the sexual politics, and economics, of post-war Vienna, what meaning did such intense male bonding have? That marriage was a tricky issue for the men around Schubert is clear. Some played around with women, like Schober; some married very late, like Vogl, some not at all, like Bauernfeld; while some, like Schubert, seem to have bemoaned the impossibility of a companionate marriage. Feminine piety was one issue ('Why don't you marry the Pope?' Schwind asked his fiancée); inadequate means another. The State, as seems clear from Rita Steblin's work, was intensely interested in marriage as the foundation of the moral and social order, forbidding it to those (including, possibly, Schubert) who were unable to demonstrate that they had the proper financial security to undertake it. The subject of Schubert's last attempt at opera, *Der Graf von Gleichen*, was bigamy, a topic that attracted the attention of the state censors but which is more plausibly an expression of dissatisfaction with the State's intrusion into marriage contracts than a coded manifesto for homosexuality, as has been suggested.

The Solomon agenda is monocular and glaringly late twentieth century in its obsessions, easily distorted into the simple assurance that Schubert was gay, even if, in Solomon's phrase, he may have 'passed through a conventional heterosexual phase'. One cannot help agreeing with Leon Botstein in the *Cambridge Companion* when he states his concern that 'the implicitly normative psychological analysis and textual exegesis now directed at Schubert's life and work – particularly with respect to issues of sexuality – continue the traditional tendency to appropriate Schubert within universalist rhetorics'. We do not yet understand the social milieu in which Schubert worked and played; and we can be certain that the sharp-edged sexual polarities of late nineteenth-century thought which have informed the agendas of liberation and repression in the twentieth century were far less distinct in the 1820s.

Psycho-sexual criticism is central to Susan Youens's work on Schubert, including her latest book on *Die schöne Müllerin*, a thorough excavation of versions of the Miller myth in German poetry and music. At the core of her understanding of Wilhelm Müller's poetic cycle, even as subtly moulded by the composer for his own musical-dramatic ends (a process on whose twists and turns Youens is acute) is an androgynous miller boy, unsettled by the flirtation of the mill girl, and threatened by the raw sexuality of the hunter. The theme of sex and death which runs through the cycle is inevitably, and rightly, associated with Schubert's contraction of syphilis in the period just before the composition of the cycle. But the possibility of social, one might even say class, anxiety in the Miller cycle is thereby obscured. One of the stories cherished by the Schubert circle was his arrival at the trials for his Vienna choir school dressed, thanks to his family's limited means, in an unsuitable pale, whitish-blue coat which made him look, as the tease went, like 'a miller's son'. Even if the story is a myth, its retelling does dramatise a truth about Schubert. His friends were socially a cut above him. He spent much of his social and professional life negotiating the narrow gulf between being patronised and receiving patronage, full in equal measure of charm and awkward, even angry discourtesy. It seems not unlikely that a cycle of poems in which a miller boy, a journeyman apprentice, woos the daughter of a mill owner, only to have her snatched from him by the free-born huntsman, would have had a personal appeal to the socially insecure miller boy in Schubert, much as the musical ironies of the hurdy-gurdy man may have drawn him irresistibly back to Müller's *Winterreise* poems.

If this is a minor footnote to interpretations of *Die schöne Müllerin*, one can go further. Only by looking at Schubert's milieu in all its specific aspects will we gain what Leon Botstein calls a 'better-differentiated sense of the universal aspects of Schubert's genius'. Schubert's Romanticism, in Robert Schumann's words, was not 'wrought from thin air'; it was constructed from the specific conditions, social, intellectual and material, of his Habsburg habitat. A city, Vienna, in which islands of abandoned rusticity floated in a sea of encroaching urbanisation; in which population and mortality were reaching fresh peaks, making the body an enemy; in which the medieval and the baroque vied in splendour. A musical culture that drew ten thousand mourners to Beethoven's funeral; that was largely nourished by a tight-knit group of state employees, materially comfortable but politically cramped; and that veered between publishers' demands for assimilable *Hausmusik* and a public craze for the diabolical virtuosity of a Paganini. Perceptions of time (the very stuff of music) were changing radically, both on the grand scale, as the new geology made its mark, and day by day, as the capitalist ethic entrenched itself. Perceptions of nature shifted too, as green spaces disappeared from an expanding city, and the rural was idealised. Schubert's letters during his summer walking tour of 1825 show him fascinated by the sublimity of the mountain landscape, an emblem of what he calls 'terrifying nature'. This terror eats its way into the songs, with an ambivalence about the natural world, which is by turns personified – as beneficent or ferociously hostile – or, in a darker vein of thought, represented as blind and unfeeling.

'Schubert', Botstein writes, 'presents a classic paradigm of how the local becomes the basis for a novel cultural formation', whose significance extends far beyond the local, though this is 'dialectically the result of its contingency on the specifics of time and place'. He is right; and further understanding of the composer will come from connecting the local and the universal, the personal and professional, and, most knotty of all, the textual and the contextual. The compulsion to relate what Leopold von Sonnleithner called his friend's 'earthly pilgrimage' to the 'spirit that comes from his music' continues. Sonnleithner's own formulation was pithy and appropriately veiled: 'Thus lived Schubert, and so he was.'

1997

Winterreise

When I am abroad in the morning I go to meet the sun,
and in the evening, when I am abroad, I follow it, till I am
down among the dead. I don't know why I told this story.
I could just as well have told another. Perhaps some other
time I'll be able to tell another. Living souls, you will see
how alike they are.

    Samuel Beckett, *The Expelled* (1946)

In 1827 Franz Schubert, the Viennese composer, discovered, in a magazine, twelve new poems by Wilhelm Müller, the Berlin poet. The two artists had never met, although Müller did briefly visit Vienna to study modern Greek. Schubert himself never left Austria, never saw the sea or visited another great city. He had already set Müller's *Liederspiel, Die schöne Müllerin* in 1824. Out of an ironic piece of rustic naivety he crafted a tragic narrative of sexual obsession and loss. Müller's poems were subtitled 'Im Winter zu lesen' (to be read in the winter), a bauble to entertain a group of like-minded friends during the dark December months. Schubert, abandoning all Müller's irony and his subtitle, made something more deeply wintry out of the material he came upon. When he discovered Müller's *Die Winterreise*, he encountered something more essentially cold and forbidding – 'dreadful' as the composer himself called it – something actually rather atypical of Müller as a poet.

Again, the composer remoulded. He dropped the definite article, making his *Winterreise* more stark, abstract and generalised in the human sense. The other crucial reshaping was accidental, but a happy accident at that. Schubert made very good use of the fact that, having set the twelve poems he came across in the journal *Urania*, he found those same poems, in a different order, embedded in a twenty-four-poem *Winterreise* of Müller's which appeared the following year, 1828. Instead of reordering his set of twelve, breaking it open and inserting the new poems in Müller's order, he retained his first part of twelve songs and then set the missing poems out of sequence. As a result any residual narrative coherence in Müller's sequence is lost, and a heightened sense of abstraction, alienation and waywardness is gained, especially in the second half, haphazardly constructed as it is, from left-overs, as it were. Only once does Schubert make a choice, changing the position of 'Mut' in the cycle, presumably in order to vary the rhythmic impetus. Schubert corrected the proofs of the final version of *Winterreise* on his deathbed.

The house in which Schubert died in November 1828, in which he made the final version of *Winterreise*, is close by the Viennese food market. You walk down the street from the bustling Naschmarkt, past retro furniture stores and shops selling old vinyl LPs and hi-fi equipment, to an early nineteenth-century apartment house, three storeys high. Two plaques, one nineteenth century, one twentieth, identify the spot. Once inside, you are transported back. Not so much by the museum which the apartment itself has become – it's too ordered – as by the courtyard and passageways that surround it. It feels as if it hasn't changed much in these nearly two hundred years – the flagstones, the brown paintwork, the well down below, the slightly seedy air. No one very important lives here.

Thousands of miles west, across the ocean, in a magnificent monument to opulent scholarship, you can call up the manuscript of *Winterreise*. You can touch the thick paper, and see for yourself the heavy scorings out (often a decisive box with cross-hatching), the first ideas and the second, the differing idiosyncratic markings in Schubert's hand which the business of publication has ironed into a sort of uniformity. Accents that stab, accents that stroke, passages written in haste, passages written more calmly. The Pierpont Morgan Library in mid-town Manhattan is a world away from the Kettenbrücken Straße in Vienna. The distance somehow represents the strange things that have happened over the past two centuries to this very strange work. It has moved from back-street post-Napoleonic Vienna to the great metropolis of global capitalism. Its first performance, by the composer, was in a private room; it can now fill the vastness of New York's iconic Carnegie Hall.

A lot of writing about *Winterreise*, a lot of my own thinking about it, has been historical and contextual. Who were Schubert's circle? What did the repression of Metternich's Vienna do to them? How did they conduct their friendships and their love affairs? What did it mean to live in the constant fear of death by infectious disease, in an age before the discovery of the microbe? What did religion really mean for these men and women? These are all issues worth thinking about when preparing to listen to *Winterreise*. But the issues that now seem more urgent to me concern the modernity of the piece, its embeddedness in twentieth-century culture and its continuing meaning for us. While he was writing one of the master texts of philosophy, the *Tractatus Logico-Philosophicus*, a hammer-blow to many nineteenth-century dreams, Ludwig Wittgenstein (brother of the pianist Paul) was, in a typically bizarre scene, taking time off to whistle *Winterreise* to the accompaniment of a close friend. *Winterreise* was a crucial work for Samuel Beckett, his hopeless alienated outcasts close companions of Schubert's wanderer. Each of us makes our own *Winterreise*, always a mark of the imperishable in art. It remains a very open-ended piece, full of interpretative choices to be made, new avenues to be explored, experiments to be tried.

Decisions about how to perform *Winterreise* have to be made. First and foremost, there is the decision to perform it at all. It was not performed as a whole, in public, until the 1850s, and its very first (private) performance was by Schubert himself, to a circle of his friends. Sometimes a performance to a paying audience can be uncomfortable, almost an invasion of privacy. But, in the end, I am convinced that *Winterreise*, however intimate it may be, is a public work, a theatrical work indeed, betrayed by its construction, one that, written at a time when notions of public and private were the site of dispute, plays with and artfully exploits our unease at the disclosure of intimacy. In this respect it is at one with much of Schubert's mature work – one thinks of the late piano sonatas – in which cosiness abuts ferocity, in which the meditative is suddenly overtaken by a passionate outburst.

To move from a grand issue like this to the mundane choices one has to make in performing *Winterreise*, a few details have to be grappled with. In terms of key, Schubert made revisions between manuscript and printed version. I usually perform the original, manuscript, high-key versions of 'Wasserflut', 'Rast' (though retaining Schubert's revised shape for the final vocal phrase of each verse), 'Mut' and 'Der Leiermann'. Schubert's reasons for transposing songs down may often have been rooted in his publisher's anxiety about what singers at home could manage (though Viennese pitch of the 1820s was probably lower than the A=440+ of today's concert halls); the higher keys are part of the original conception and, in the case of 'Der Leiermann', a very different effect is conjured up by the B minor originally planned. Which is not to say it is to be preferred. Such decisions are a mixture of the pragmatic (speaking as a tenor) and the aesthetic. Key relationships in *Winterreise* are part of its architecture and not to be disregarded. At the same time, the tessitura of the cycle wanders between the tenor and the high baritone, ideal for neither. Transposition away from the final printed version is almost always necessary; tenors have the luxury of 'transpositions' Schubert himself retrospectively supplied. Which makes it odd that *Winterreise* has so often been seen as ideally a bass or baritone cycle, a perception rooted in some notion of the darkness of the work. It is dark, of course, but it is full of defiance and bitterness, gallows humour and sharp irony (how different from *Die schöne Müllerin*, where Schubert had excised the poet's irony) – a young man's work, a world away from the bass realm of the *Vier ernste Gesänge*. I should add that I more usually perform the revised version of the twelfth song, 'Einsamkeit', because Schubert's transposition here was clearly connected to his decision to add twelve more songs to complete his *Winterreise*. When, occasionally, performing the twelve-song Ur-*Winterreise* as a self-contained work (often in recital with Britten's great cycle, *Winter Words*), I return to the manuscript, beginning and ending the truncated cycle in the same key.

Two more textual issues arise. The rhythm of the piano's first phrase in 'Wasserflut' is a vexed issue: should one smoothly assimilate the dotted quaver and semi-quaver rhythm in the left hand to the triplet in the right, or adopt the alternative dissociating strategy that Alfred Brendel has dismissed as an inappropriate 'Brahmsian polyrhythm', unavailable as a musical device in the 1820s? Whatever the academic rights and wrongs (and the jury is still out on this issue in musical notation), trial and error have convinced me that it works, both as a sort of recapitulation of the same rhythmic motif in the penultimate vocal bar of 'Der Linden-baum' and, simply, as an expressive device. The staccato triplets in the left hand in the first section of the first verse of 'Frühlingstraum', which Leif Ove Andsnes plays in our 2004 recording of the cycle, come from a version of the song that Schubert went on to revise. We discovered this version in the critical edition when we were making the recording; it seemed to reflect one particular aspect of the song, one truth among many, and we decided to go with it. As musicologists will tell you, the idea of *Werktreue*, or scrupulous adherence to a composer's written instructions, was quite a late development in the nineteenth century.

Winterreise was not the first great song-cycle – Beethoven's *An die ferne Geliebte* and Schubert's own *Die schöne Müllerin* precede it – but it is the work that definitively placed the Lied at the centre of the great musical tradition. In terms of sheer length, *Winterreise* is prodigious – is there any longer repertory work performed in recital without interval? – and its lack of formal musical unity (a unity that *An die ferne Geliebte* maintains) was surely an example to the fragmentary aesthetic of the musical Romantics. At the same time, the long strophic sequences of *Die schöne Müllerin*, with their naive folkloric element, are replaced by far more use of through-composition. Even a song such as 'Der Lindenbaum', so often extracted from the cycle or sung in unison as a folksong, is a sophisticated play on memory using rhythm and modulation to evoke the moods and tenses of the poem; and it is bound together with its predecessor song, 'Erstarrung', by a common motif, trans- formed as between the last bar of the one and the first bar of the other, but still recognisable. Throughout the cycle fragmentary echoes and reminiscences evoke a mind full of regret but still pulsing with life, often solipsistic but at the same time alert to the external world and to the play of verbal meaning and musical gesture. This is *Winterreise*'s genius, and the reason it speaks to us now as it spoke to the generation of its creator.

2004

Die schöne Müllerin
(Im Winter zu lesen)

It is not the latest slight – which in itself is minimal – that produces the fit of crying, the outburst of despair or the attempt at suicide, in disregard of the axiom that an effect must be proportionate to its cause; the small slight of the present moment has aroused and set working the memories of very many, more intense, earlier slights, behind all of which there lies in addition the memory of a serious slight in childhood which has never been overcome.

Sigmund Freud, *The Aetiology of Hysteria* (1896)

At first sight, *Die schöne Müllerin* is a far less unsettling work than *Winterreise*. It tells a story, clearly, with a narrative structure that allows for joy and musing in equal measure, the whirr of the mill-wheel and the purling of the companionate brook. How much more forbidding is the winter's journey, with its manic-depressive trajectory and open-ended conclusion, how modern.

Die schöne Müllerin emerged from a long tradition of related stories, and is less quintessentially Romantic than *Winterreise*. Wandering in the latter is existential, unsettled, compulsive; in the former it starts out as the simple journeyman's search for employment and is, apparently, a thing of joy. 'Das Wandern ist des Müllers Lust', we are asked to believe, and we sort of do. There are plenty of fairy-tales about apprentices setting out with a song in their heart (though often with a curse from their old mother ringing in their ears); Narcissus myths about the dangers of overmuch reflection; and folk-tales grounded in the old conflict

165

between settled ways of life and the rootless huntsman, the smooth and the hairy – all the way back to Jacob and Esau. Closer to the Biedermeier era, there had been a real literary trend for tales about millers and huntsmen and mill-girls – something Wilhelm Müller, the poet of *Die schöne Müllerin*, drew on and intermittently mocked.

Schubert was no naive co-opter of all this cultural baggage. Just as Müller's *Die Winterreise* became Schubert's *Winterreise* (dropping the definite article), with a corresponding loss of narrative coherence and intensification of aesthetic power, *Die schöne Müllerin* (ultimately part of the same collection of poems) was utterly transformed at the composer's hands. And, as ever, he knew what he was doing (something the Schubert industry, with its image of the composer as a cosy anti-Beethoven, was at pains to deny). What had been, quite literally, a game, poetical charades played at home by knowing literary types, became deadly serious. It would be all too easy to see this as the simple-minded composer sentimentalising his material. The reverse is nearer the truth. The original *Müllerin*, in its equivocation between naive feeling and irony, exemplifies Oscar Wilde's *bon mot* that sentimentality is the bank holiday of cynicism. Schubert's cycle removes the poet's ironic voice, and minimises the presence of the girl herself. 'Es kommt ein Regen' is one of only two things she says (the other expresses her love of the colour green), and how brilliant of Schubert to hit on a remark so thoroughly ambiguous – a cold rehearsal of fact, or a piece of heartless mockery, teasing the boy for his tears? In doing so, he creates a piece with the resonance of myth, which can play to the unconscious and draw on deep-seated notions of sexual fear, narcissism, a shying away from adulthood, even class antagonism between the indentured and the hunting free.

Die schöne Müllerin was the first Schubert cycle – perhaps the first song-cycle – that I fell in love with, and it is easy to see its appeal to the adolescent mind: a story of disappointed love, a young innocent defeated by a more experienced, more glamorous, presumably older rival. In fact, as with so much of Schubert's music, it has been all too easy to privilege the biographical. Commentators have been doing this with regularity since Schubert's own time, and they have yet to let up. The assumption is of a naive artist pouring his feelings into artless melody. Nothing could be further from the truth. Schubert was a radical composer, and *Die schöne Müllerin* is not a work in which we should make the all-too-common mistake of equating creator with protagonist, either in the old version – poor Schubert, disappointed in love, shy with the girls – or the new – Schubert the homosexual *avant la lettre*, drawn to a story about an androgynous youth who never really wanted the girl anyway and who is defined in precise opposition to the priapic, hirsute masculinity of the hunter. Schubert did make a very clear decision to remove the framing device of Wilhelm Müller's poetic cycle, purging the work of ironic commentary – a decision of a piece with tinier but significant alterations he made even to classic literary texts that he set to music – but this does not entail simple identification with the first-person narrative. The boy's failure really to dare to address the girl, after all, contains its own complex of ironies – a central song, 'Pause', in which the miller declares that his heart is too full to go on singing. He sings on nevertheless, and sings himself into oblivion.

Die schöne Müllerin is one of the central works of the

European classical tradition because, despite its cosy setting, it plumbs the psychoanalytic depths, speaking of sex and death in a way few other works have managed, achieving a perfect balance between stasis and movement which lends its tragic unfolding an extraordinarily compulsive quality. It stands with the later works of 1827–8 – the string quintet, *Winterreise*, the last three piano sonatas, the songs that go to make up *Schwanengesang* – as a sort of artistic miracle. From the outset, Schubert's work was saturated with love and death – one of his earliest songs is entitled 'Leichenfantasie' (corpse fantasy) – a result of personal history, poetic taste and cultural milieu. Schubert's private tragedies in 1823, the year of *Die schöne Müllerin* – diagnosis of syphilis, time spent in hospital, a future curtailed – will have interacted, in a complex but undeniable manner, with the genesis of this very public utterance, in which charm, obsession, beauty and savagery battle for the mind of the listener.

2005

Hugo Wolf

It is hard to credit, but Hugo Wolf is still an underrated composer. Known for his songs, he is seen as the province of the aficionado, a minority taste, a footnote to late Romanticism. It's true that his opera, *Der Corregidor*, rejected for the Vienna Opera by its director Gustav Mahler, is a curiosity; that the symphonic poem, *Penthesilea*, with its ever so fin-de-siècle woman-fearing tale of an Amazonian queen, is flawed; and that only the *Italian Serenade* is much played. He didn't write successfully on a grand scale, or without words. Yet, in the Lieder repertoire, he is every bit the equal of his great predecessors, Schubert and Schumann. The self-conscious mastery of a miniaturist form – in the age of *japonisme* or of Chekhov's short stories – may well have been a response to Wagnerian gigantism. As Nietzsche put it, while recovering from his intoxication with Wagner: 'What can be done well today, what can be masterly, is only what is small.'

Wolf, too, had been drunk on Wagner, and in the culture wars of his day it was clear where he stood: with the Wagnerians. Yet if many of the songs are harmonically full of Wagnerian sensuality, some of them dominated by the sort of declamation that Mahler, for one, hated, others are tuneful, simple and essentially lyric. In the best of them, Wolf fused together Wagner's ineffable evocation of longing with Schumann's genius for what he called *Seelen-* or *Tongemälde* (mood or scene painting). In a song such as 'Nachtzauber' (night magic) we have all the sensuality of

Wagner's endless melody, without the endlessness. When, after a two-year period of creative sterility, Wolf went back to writing songs in 1895, his motto was encapsulated in the first song of the *Italian Songbook* – 'Auch kleine Dinge können uns entzücken' (even small things can delight us).

The outline of Wolf's composing career is a distillation of the manic creativity and Romantic attraction to extremes that one sees in the songwriting careers of Schubert and Schumann. Schubert wrote songs in bursts, on the back of restaurant menus, when the mood took him, or when a particular poet's work seized him; it's probably true to say that all Schumann's most famous songs were written in one emotionally momentous year, that of his marriage, 1840. Wolf, similarly, composed songs like one possessed. Between 1888 and 1891 he wrote more than two hundred, including the Mörike, Eichendorff and Goethe songbooks, which strive to encapsulate in music the word-hoard of those three poetic masters. In periods of creativity he could write two or three songs a day. The opening song of the Mörike set, 'Der Genesene an die Hoffnung' ('The Convalescent addressing Hope') is an overt recognition of composition as pathology, a celebration of a release from artistic incapacity but somehow, also, an anticipation of the Wolf who stares at us, terrifying and terrified, in a chilling photograph taken in the mental asylum in Vienna where he died in 1903 at the age of forty-two.

In the days of optimism before his breakdown, his enthusiasm was infectious. Letters to friends bubbled over with the sheer excitement of having found a musical language and of writing at full tilt. 'Eventually, after a lot of groping around, the button came undone'; that's how Wolf himself expressed the sense of release. We hear his joy and the excitement in much of the music. There's the light-hearted, syncopated tread of 'Auf einer Wanderung' ('On a Journey') as the poet arrives in town ready for love; the critic being kicked down the stairs in 'Abschied' ('Farewell') to the strains of a drunken, ecstatic Viennese waltz; the boisterous roister-doister of 'Seemanns Abschied' ('Sailor's Farewell').

If there is plenty of Wagnerian eroticism at work in Wolf's output – in the delayed climaxes of 'Ganymed', in the central group of the Mörike set whose songs weave together the sacred with the sexual – elsewhere the composer can indulge in self-conscious mockery of it. The title 'Nimmersatte Liebe' ('Insatiable Love') is immediately undercut by a teasing piano introduction and, despite the intervening chromatic treatment of the pains of passion (girls are like lambs under the knife, the poet tells us), it all ends, as Wolf put it in a letter to a friend, by breaking out 'into a right old student's song, damned merry'. Singing it nowadays in concert, it almost seems like a chimerical cabaret turn, half Richard Wagner, half Noël Coward.

My first experience of Hugo Wolf was as a child, hearing 'Verschwiegene Liebe' ('Silent Love') on Barbra Streisand's *Classical Barbra* album (much praised by both Leonard Bernstein and Glenn Gould). I remembered the song years later, and it drew me back to Wolf. Thank you, Barbra (and my brother Mark, whose LP it was). In essence, the story ought to be one of boundaries broken down, of how vocal traditions can circulate and cross-fertilise. But, in fact, thirty years on, listening again to that track with Tony Pappano, while we were making a recording of Wolf songs, we agreed in sensing how reverential and cautious Streisand is with the classical repertoire. If you go back and listen to the early recordings of Wolf from the 1930s, put out by the Hugo Wolf Society and bought by music-lovers on subscription, the first sensation is of an old world, of something unfamiliar. Then you start to hear the sheer variety of vocal styles among the various singers, and the sense of freedom. That's what one strives for in singing this music today: an interpretative freedom that can draw inspiration, if not technique, as much from popular vocalists such as Billie Holiday or Bob Dylan as from the operatic tradition. Wolf's songs are about modulating music with words, and vice versa, something that great popular vocalists are masters of. Classical singers have a lot to learn from the best of them.

2006

Janáček

The sex lives of the great composers seem to command a disproportionate amount of interest. It's as if the sheer inexplicable passion of an essentially Romantic, expressive art has to be matched by some personal story of secret, mysterious and hence unfathomable passion; as if the abstractness of music must be mediated by the fascination of the flesh.

Schubert's sexuality is the subject of unending and irresoluble debate; the troubling issue of Benjamin Britten's alleged paedophile tendencies remains obsessive; while the destroyed letters between Brahms and his late mentor's widow, Clara Schumann, provide infinite non-existent material for the prurient. All too often, the interest boils down to the speculative and usually unanswerable: did they or didn't they?

Biographical criticism has incurred some critical opprobrium over the years (the death of the author and all that) but seems to be in rude health, none the less. As a performer it is a more practical business. Musicians need food for their interpretations, and the personal circumstances of a work's composition can usefully form part of one's imaginative diet.

When I first became involved in performing Leoš Janáček's *The Diary of One Who Vanished* five years ago – and since then I've acted it in English, recorded it in Czech and just finished making a BBC4 documentary about it – the rehearsal process involved all sorts of connected ephemera, from Janáček's love life to the ploughing technique of the piece's peasant protagonist, something I experimented with in a Berkshire field.

The Diary of One Who Vanished is a weird, hybrid, uncategorisable work. Janáček, who was born a hundred and fifty years ago this year, is best known as a composer of great operas: *Kátya Kabanová, The Makropoulos Case, Jenůfa*.

The *Diary* can be seen as a sort of miniature opera, a dramatic cantata for tenor, mezzo-soprano, piano and a small female chorus that, at the crux of the action, seems to emerge from the very air. Or it can be thought of as a song-cycle gone wrong, its moaning peasant protagonist first cousin to Schubert's miller boy in *Die schöne Müllerin*, rescued from apparently inevitable lovesick annihilation by the irruption of a sexy Gypsy mezzo-soprano into his field.

When I first heard of it, in complete ignorance of Janáček or his oeuvre, I thought it must be political (that 'vanished'), something about show trials and unjust imprisonment. It turned out that it is, indeed, a work about freedom, but of a very different sort. Setting a group of poems published as authentic in a Brno newspaper, it tells of a love affair between a Moravian peasant boy and a Gypsy. The freedom it celebrates is personal freedom: the freedom to love without social interference, to cross class, culture and ethnicity in search of completeness.

At the same time, the music that tells the story is saturated with sadness at what has to be left behind in the search for fulfilment. It is a love story that leaves one with an intense sense of loneliness as the protagonist says goodbye to family and home to follow his Gypsy destiny.

It was because of my long-term involvement with the piece, and my previous career as an academic historian, that I became involved in making a documentary on

Janáček for BBC4. It was a strange business for me. Billed as a sort of detective story, it takes me to Moravia to explore the two mysteries of the work – the true provenance of the poems that Janáček set, and the nature of his own relationship with Kamila Stösslová, the woman who inspired *The Diary*, and indeed most of the remaining masterpieces of the composer's life.

Travelling through rural Moravia, one acute impression was the sheer concentration of provincial talent in the latter days of Habsburg rule – we drove in quick succession through the villages where Freud, Mahler and Janáček were born. Janáček was a choirboy in the abbey where Gregor Mendel planted peas to found the science of genetics, and played the organ at his funeral.

Yet what kept coming back to me was my own previous job as a television researcher and how much, in that role, I had shied away from asking the intellectually disreputable but journalistically crucial nitty-gritty. The embarrassing questions – in the case of Janáček and Kamila, did they or didn't they have a sexual relationship?

I met Kamila's son, Otto, an extraordinarily unbowed, amused and amusing survivor of Nazism and Czech communism who died only a few months ago. His view of Janáček was distinctly unromantic: he remembered his mother threatening to leave if the old man didn't stop making a racket on the harmonium (a.k.a. playing his music) on their last visit to him. Janáček's British biographer, John Tyrrell, thinks the Kamila relationship was based in fantasy; a Czech scholar remembers a letter he saw in the 1970s, since disappeared, that might suggest otherwise. It was certainly an obsession for Janáček – over six hundred letters survive, passionate outpourings.

In the end, Janáček's fantasy remains far more important than the unknowable facts. He was, by the time he met Kamila, a man in his sixties, unhappily married, his two children dead. A provincial, marginal figure for much of his early and middle life, he had suddenly become a cultural icon after the Vienna premiere of his opera *Jenůfa* in 1916.

The Diary, begun in 1917, was a watershed in his artistic career. It was an experimental piece of idiosyncratic modernism based on a newspaper report. It was also a musical and dramatic expression of his falling in love with Kamila, whom he called his Gypsy.

Whatever the reality of their relationship (she was happily married with two sons, a woman in her twenties, musically uneducated), Kamila was the muse who inspired almost all the works of his late years. Schubert's confrontation with syphilis and mortality unleashed a flood of late works; Kamila did the same for Janáček, who had been less fertile in the years between the Brno premiere of *Jenůfa* and its Viennese triumph. Kamila was a romantic, erotic focus for the renewal of energy that public recognition brought.

Kamila inadvertently seized Janáček's attention when he heard her. Sitting in a cafe in a Moravian spa, before he'd even met her, he sketched the musical shape of her voice in a notebook. Ten years or so later, just before his death, he filled another album with skeletal musical fragments centred around the idea of Kamila and her impending visit to him with her sons.

She was, because of that trip, with him when he died. This lent his latter years a sort of aesthetic shape which he had already attempted to formalise by making Kamila his heir, an effort the Brno courts rejected. She nevertheless received a proportion of the royalties from the works she had inspired.

It's telling, I think, that the voice came first. Janáček's musical creativity needed an immersion in humanity, in emotion, in flesh and blood, to sustain it. In that sense, he was a world away from the mainstream of German modernism (Schoenberg, Webern *et al.*) or the success story of international eclecticism, Stravinsky, for whom music was about music, not really an expressive art-form at all. Stravinsky wrote few songs, and his one opera, *The Rake's Progress*, brilliant and moving as it can be in parts, remains cumulatively cold and detached.

If Janáček's music lives with an extraordinary power and urgency, it is because he bucked the trend of musical abstraction. He did so because he couldn't avoid it, because it was in his temperament to confuse the personal and the aesthetic. This is something of an intellectual puzzle – how, after all, do we turn feelings into music? – and, at the same time, an artistic miracle.

2004

Staging Janáček's Diary *in 1999 was one of the most exciting experiences of my working life. Directed by Deborah Warner, translated by Seamus Heaney, with the mezzo-soprano Ruby Philogene as the Gypsy and Julius Drake as musical director, it was a co-production between ENO, the Holland and Munich Festivals, the Lincoln Center, the Abbey Theatre, Dublin, and the National Theatre in London. Much of the rehearsal period – five weeks for a piece lasting about thirty-five minutes – involved exploring the boundaries between concert and theatre. Here's what I wrote in the programme at the time:*

Diary of One Who Vanished: Escape from the song-cycle?

Song-cycles were my way into grown-up singing; but, as with most singers today, opera has become a vital part of my life, and it was opera that forced me into becoming a full-time singer. Thus the strange fascination of *Diary of One Who Vanished*. A hybrid – part opera, part song-cycle – it appeared just at the time, around the First World War, when the song recital was crystallising into its current form.

By 1920 concert gear, concert layout, concert lighting, even concert programming, had largely assumed the form we know from today's Wigmore Hall. The barely imaginable proposed reforms of the late Romantic period had fizzled out (coloured mood lighting and incense burners; plants and palms concealing performers; the singer dressed as 'Apollonian priest' or 'singer of Bacchus') and a singleness of purpose, a primarily musical or even vocal focus had emerged.

What we have today in song recitals is a highly artificial form. Evening dress of the mid- to late nineteenth century is put on in order to perform music largely written in the same period or just before. Formality has triumphed. Music at least initially conceived for a primarily domestic or convivial arena, poetry written for home theatricals (the lyrics of Schubert's *Die schöne Müllerin*, for instance) have been co-opted into the sacred realm of the concert hall. At the same time, the very artificiality of the form, its formal restrictions – the small area of stage available to the singer, the economy of gesture, the single curvilinear prop (the piano lid) – perversely allows tiny ruptures of the rules to count for much.

Diary, on the other hand, explodes all the rules, and quite deliberately. It sets out as a Schubertian journey, the Moravian equivalent of the Austro-German Lieder classics, *Die schöne Müllerin* or Mahler's *Lieder eines fahrenden Gesellen*. Young innocent working man falls hopelessly in love with bewitching minx. There is common ground between Janáček's Janek the ploughman and Schubert's miller boy not only in the realm of musical lyricism (a feature often underplayed) but also in their exaggerated fear of adult sexuality. Schubert's journeyman miller finds the mill girl's flirtation perplexing, while the supercharged testosterone of his rival, the huntsman, is a patent threat. Janáček's ploughboy pushes this even further: appropriating the stock images of female sexual ruination, he weeps for the loss of his own virtue.

But the cycle doesn't stop at that point, doesn't end in suicide, in Romantic denial. Instead, Janek discovers his sexuality and, arguably, finds sexual fulfilment in the arms of his Gypsy girl. The Lieder tradition is turned upside down. Written by a Czech former subject of the Austro-Hungarian dual monarchy, *Diary* subverts the conventions of the German song-cycle (so rooted in German linguistic nationalism) by the simplest of devices. Somebody, a woman, a stateless person, interrupts the hero halfway through his sad story. Seeking and offering freedom, her rescuing of Janek from the song-cycle itself remains a powerful metaphor.

The Threepenny Opera

The counter-intuitive notion of doing *The Threepenny Opera* with trained voices, opera singers if you like, came to me when I was doing Lieder recitals with my friends Dorothea Röschmann, Angelika Kirchschlager and Tommy Quasthoff. I simply heard them, in my mind's ear, singing this music and thought, how wonderful would that be. It's partly a question of a Lieder singer's commitment to the words, of vocal character, of a vocal quality that I hadn't heard in this piece before and that I'm hearing now, in rehearsal with the *echt* Weill expert, H. K. Gruber. But I think there are also deeper reasons for giving a performance like this, once in a while or more often, with singers like this; reasons to go against the grain of the Brecht tradition in which the rasp and the snarl cloud the beauty of Weill's music. There's room, in any performance, for both, grit and *cantilena* and, hearing Röschmann sing 'Pirate Jenny', or Kirchschlager the 'Solomon Song', you'll know what I mean.

The Threepenny Opera is one of those accidental masterpieces. Argued over by cast and creators, teetering on the edge of disaster, its final form or content undefined right up to its opening in 1928, it was then the smash hit of the era, a theatrical totem of the Weimar Republic.

Yet, as the work that made Bertolt Brecht world-famous, it's not clear how much of it he was really responsible for. Many of the best, most characteristic ideas, right down to the title itself – Brecht's original was the less engaging *Scum* – came from others. The piece started out as an adaptation of John Gay's early eighteenth-century satire, *The Beggar's Opera*. Much, if not most, of Brecht's text has been convincingly, if controversially, attributed to his collaborator and lover Elisabeth Hauptmann; and some of its finest song lyrics are pastiche Kipling, or lifted word-for-word from the poetry of the French medieval writer François Villon, in somebody else's translation.

It is less the text than the composer Kurt Weill's music that has captured the imagination of successive generations. Well beyond the never-ending cover versions of the 'Ballad of Mack the Knife' by the likes of Louis Armstrong or Sting, it has defined a whole notion of rough style which continues to inform the rock aesthetic. In this sense, it hardly matters what Brecht's precise contribution was, musically or poetically, because the spirit of this leather-clad, posturing, narcissistic genius – the perfect rock star *avant la lettre* – hovers over the entire enterprise. Bob Dylan's response was alert, loving these 'songs with tough language', which he first heard in the early 1960s, finding them 'erratic, unrhythmical and herky-jerky', full of 'weird visions'. The singers were 'thieves, scavengers or scallywags and they all roared and snarled'. 'They were like folk-songs in nature,' Dylan perceptively wrote, 'but unlike folk-songs, too, because they were sophisticated.'

I first got to know *The Threepenny Opera* at school and directed it at university in the 1980s (my Mack the Knife is now a prominent Labour MP). This was a period of political and social polarisation, one of those rare epochs in modern British history when the class interest of the state had been (however tentatively) unmasked. As miners were on strike, police were massing on the picket lines. In such times, a piece that depicted criminals as aspirant bourgeois, and vice versa, that placed an ethical materialism ('food first, then morality') at the centre of its social agenda, had a visceral appeal.

In the meantime we've had an age of luxuriant materialism in which Mack the Knife – a slickly dressed gangster-capitalist shark who sings a champagne-fuelled 'Ballad of the Good Life' – would have felt quite at home, followed by a earth-shattering financial crash which takes us right back to the piece's roots in Gay's Augustan satire and the South Sea Bubble. *The Threepenny Opera* is always, one way or another, preternaturally relevant.

But, reading the script now, learning the lyrics afresh, I am struck by the ferocity of casual violence, the bleakness of its vision of sexual relations, the coarseness of the language, the cynicism at work despite the occasional progressive catchphrase. This is a piece that was forged in the extraordinary aftermath of the First World War, the slow strangulation of the liberal ideal, the apotheosis of violence in politics on the left and right.

Theatrically, that violence creates an enormous energy; but with the music, something more complicated is going on. Brecht, the arch anti-sentimentalist, builds his love duet for Mack the Knife and Polly Peachum on the ironic lines 'Love will last or not, in this place or that'; yet Weill sets it to music of surpassing, if fragile, casual beauty. Overall, Weill's score swells, despite the cynical edge, with an enormous sense of longing and poignancy. It confronts hollowness, engages with despair, in a way that the Brechtian script, in its brisk, anarchic, brutal, absurdist comedy, on the whole does not.

Weill's aims and motives are as unclear as the genesis of *The Threepenny Opera* itself, but in the context of his whole career, which ended with Broadway musicals in exile, his essential Romanticism is worth bearing in mind. Weimar objectivity shouldn't obscure this. In its interweaving of musical invention and emotional response, in its grappling with the question of how song relates to action, *The Threepenny Opera* is as much part of the classical mainstream as Monteverdi's *Orfeo* or Puccini's *Madama Butterfly*.

2009

Noël Coward

Nearly thirty years after Noël Coward's death, his reputation as a dramatist stands at a new peak. Received into the great tradition of English comedy, he is now seen as a precursor of Beckett and Pinter. *Private Lives*, triumphantly revived by Howard Davies in London and New York last season, is recognised as part of the great tradition of world theatre.

The Coward legend has had its ups and downs. Born in Middlesex in 1899, theatre's golden boy moved without missing a beat from the brittle world-weariness of the 1920s, through 1930s nostalgia to the patriotic endeavours of the Second World War. But in the 1950s his blend of insouciance and sentimentality lost favour at home. The bruised patriot became a tax exile, finding new fame as lounge-lizard cabaret performer. Yet in the mid-1960s Coward's time came around again and *Hay Fever* became the first revival of a living author's work at the National Theatre, directed by the author.

At the same time Coward has always been recognised as a talented songwriter. His own musical credentials were, like those of many popular songwriters, wayward. This was the man who could play the piano in only three keys, E flat, B flat and A flat, declaring that 'the sight of two sharps frightens me to death'; who after a visit to Glyndebourne characterised Mozart's music as 'like piddling on flannel'; and who once conversed with a bemused Sibelius under the impression that he was Delius. But the highbrows of the period loved his music. Some of the songs in the revue *This Year of Grace* 'struck me on the forehead like a bullet', wrote Virginia Woolf.

In the long run, though, the judgement of another high-brow, Cyril Connolly, has maybe had the edge, at least as far as the songs are concerned. He believed that Coward's 'very adaptability . . . makes him inferior to a more compact and worldly competitor in his own sphere, like Cole Porter'. Coward's range as a composer was certainly remarkable, and in making a selection of his songs from the 1920s and 1930s for a recording I have been struck by the sheer variety of genre. They range from those that have become jazz standards, such as 'Twentieth Century Blues', via the satirical patter of 'Mad Dogs and Englishmen', to the perfumed wistfulness of numbers from the operetta *Bitter Sweet*, such as 'Zigeuner' or 'If Only You Could Come with Me'.

The question of Coward's stature as a tunesmith is, in the end, a subjective one; it may be that the melodic subtlety of his songs, their harmonic twists and turns, makes them more perishable than the great standards of the American tradition. But I would maintain that Coward is closer to the Continental traditions of the time than the American comparison allows. I would also argue that music stands at the centre of Coward's art and cannot be ignored as if he were a brilliant playwright who just happened to write a few famous songs.

Coward often has something of an English Kurt Weill about him. The sublimated aggression of 'Mad Dogs and Englishmen', despite its blimpish cheeriness, is reminiscent of *The Threepenny Opera*'s 'Kanonen Song'. The cold wistfulness of 'Let's Say Goodbye' harks back to Macheath's and Polly's farewell in that same work. There's the same fascination with, resistance to, and ultimate embrace by American culture.

But perhaps the clearest contrast and comparison can be gathered from the superbly iconoclastic ending to Coward's patriotic pageant, *Cavalcade*. As the play reaches its ideological climax, in which one of the characters reassigns a positive value to the aftermath of the Great War – toasting 'the spirit of gallantry and courage that made a strange heaven out of unbelievable hell' – the lights fade and we cut to a scene of nightclub chaos, 1930, the decoration 'angular and strange', the song, 'Twentieth Century Blues', 'oddly discordant'.

The 'dull dancing of habit' is juxtaposed with 'six incurables in blue hospital uniform – making baskets'. A jazz band plays 'wildly'. These contrasted visions

are repeated quicker and quicker – noise grows louder and louder . . . until the general effect is complete chaos. Suddenly it all fades into darkness and silence and away at the back a Union Jack glows through the blackness. The lights slowly come up and the whole stage is composed of massive tiers, upon which stand the entire company. The Union Jack flies over their heads as they sing God Save the King.

Where Brecht and Weill in *The Threepenny Opera* typically inserted moments of sentiment into their radical parade of cynicism, Coward here does the reverse, strengthening his conservative vision with this moment of daring anarchy.

In *Private Lives*, his acknowledged masterpiece, music has a crucial role, bearing the emotional weight of the piece when the brilliant, brittle dialogue cannot carry it. The recently divorced Amanda and Elyot, heroic bickerers, find themselves in adjoining hotel rooms while honeymooning with their new spouses. The soundtrack to their re-entanglement is Coward's wonderful romantic duet 'Someday I'll Find You'. Elyot (played by Coward himself in the first production) famously scorns the song as a 'nasty insistent little tune'; but it is Amanda who has the measure of its power and its importance in the drama they are playing out: 'Extraordinary how potent cheap music is.'

The same trick is played in *Blithe Spirit* a decade later: in a ghostly reworking of Amanda's and Elyot's reunion, it is popular music, and Irving Berlin's 'Always' in particular, that summons the dead Elvira back to haunt Charles Condomine. Music in Coward's work has an access to the unconscious. 'Are you susceptible to music?' asks Judith of Richard in *Hay Fever*, Coward's first comic hit. 'I'm afraid I don't know very much about it,' he says, to which she replies: 'You probably are, then.'

Coward's music is not incidental or peripheral but central to his art, and in a proper appreciation of Coward we have to reckon with words and music – as it happens, the title of a 1932 Coward–Cochran revue. The challenge for the classical musician is to recognise the potency of so-called 'cheap music'. The Western academic classical tradition is so concerned with form and abstraction that the power of context and of performance itself to lift apparently artless material is often lost. Yet very often it is the simplest moments in classical music that achieve the heights of sublimity. Coward may not be Schubert, but he's not a million miles away.

2002

The Battle of Britten

Review of Paul Kildea, *Selling Britten*, Paul Kildea (ed.),
Britten on Music; Graham Johnson, *Britten, Voice
and Piano*, and David Matthews, *Britten*

Benjamin Britten has been a curiously contested figure
in British musical life since his first professional excur-
sions of the 1930s. What Igor Stravinsky called 'the Battle
of Britten' has been fought and refought in almost every
subsequent decade. The introduction to Paul Kildea's
indispensable collection of writings and transcripts, *Britten
on Music*, refers to a recent spat in this debate, as Philip
Hensher, critic, novelist and librettist, condemns Britten's
most popular work, the 1962 *War Requiem* (two hundred
thousand copies of the composer's recording sold in the first
year, to get down to the commercial nitty-gritty). Here's
how the exchange with Sue MacGregor, on Radio 4's *Today*
programme, went:

HENSHER: What people are really listening to is the sentiment and
not actually the quality of the music, I think, which is actually not
that high.
MACGREGOR: And you think Benjamin Britten's reputation really
doesn't extend very greatly beyond our shores?
HENSHER: I think that's true. I mean it's noticeable that most of Britten's pieces that are still popular are not the kind of abstract pieces,
not the concert pieces, but the pieces with some sort of meaning to
them ...

This hurried early-morning debate encapsulates a whole
cluster of modernist prejudices about music, and one side

of the persistent British mistrust of our greatest modern composer. The highbrows find Britten too lowbrow.

At the same time, from the other side, there is a ready assumption by many that Britten's music is too difficult, a view that performers still regularly encounter, and which even metropolitan opera houses find reflected in projected ticket sales for, say, *Billy Budd* (1951), Britten's grand-opera masterpiece. Yet it is my suspicion that a composer who so offends both sides of the debate about contemporary music and its loss of relevance must be doing something right.

It is certainly absolutely false that Britten's reputation is restricted to his homeland. A Britten season that I programmed in the Philharmonie in Cologne this year – well attended and critically acclaimed – drew together a cosmopolitan band of enthusiastic and distinguished musicians for whom Britten is a canonical figure (a French oboist to play the *Six Metamorphoses after Ovid*; a German violist to play the *Lachrymae* variations on a song by Dowland; a German soprano to sing the Pushkin settings originally written for Vishnevskaya and Rostropovich). A record label based in Paris, Virgin Classics, headed by a veteran French record executive, Alain Lanceron, is intent on producing a complete Britten edition. His operas play all over the world; I remember The Royal Opera's production of Britten's greatest opera, *The Turn of the Screw*, being a hot ticket and critical success in Paris in 1998 and the interest is now, if anything, greater. Italian audiences love the *Seven Sonnets of Michelangelo* (I've sung them in Rome, Milan, Venice and Turin), relishing Britten's grasp of their *italianità*, despite the occasionally eccentric setting of the actual Italian.

Since 1994, I have sung the *War Requiem* dozens of times, in cities such as Berlin, Dresden, Copenhagen, Lisbon, Paris,

Boston, New York, Chicago, Los Angeles and London; cities that were bombed, cities that weren't. While the response in Freiburg on the fiftieth anniversary of the bombing of that city may have had a particular quality, the piece seems to have a universal resonance. For myself, after all those performances, the singular brilliance of construction, of which so many Britten critics have always, bizarrely, complained – that telling alternation of the Latin requiem mass and Wilfred Owen's poems – never palls. For the rest, one can immerse oneself in the flow of never-dimming inspiration from Britten's own original genius and the music of the past: Verdi, very obviously, but Bach and even a little Kurt Weill, too. War is a big enough subject in itself; but the *War Requiem* is a great enough piece to reach out, beyond its occasional significance (the consecration of the new Coventry Cathedral in 1963), to speak to us more generally of death, time and loss. It is arguably the only classical composition written after 1945 to have had a continuous place in audience affections, and a growing place in the repertoire.

Hensher's judgements spring from the dominant Stravinskian aesthetic in musicology, and it is important to understand the source of the Russian master's objections. As far as his specific response to Britten is concerned, it would be hard to avoid ascribing it to the sheer paranoid envy of one generation's dominant figure for his successor. Of course, there is something fantastical about the composer of *The Rite of Spring* and *Petrushka*, the legend in his own lifetime, envying the upstart Britten; but David Matthews, in his *Britten*, a perceptive short introduction to the life and work, gives us the evidence for the prosecution. If *The Rake's Progress* is Stravinsky's answer to Britten's operatic success in general and to his realisation of *The Beggar's Opera* in particular, there are numerous other echoes and imitations, too many to be accidental. The 'Lyke-wake Dirge' of Britten's *Serenade* is set in Stravinsky's *Cantata*; *Noye's Fludde* was followed by *The Flood* from Stravinsky; both men set the story of Abraham and Isaac, Britten in medieval English, Stravinsky in a rather intimidating Hebrew. It's a measure of Britten's genius that it is by no means clear who won this battle of the scores. And certainly, as an operatic composer, despite the musical riches of the *Rake* and the adoption of Britten's most brilliant collaborator, Auden, as librettist, Britten stands far above Stravinsky.

For the truth is that if Stravinsky's aesthetic had held together logically, he ought never to have written an opera. His self-consciously perverse maintenance that music couldn't express anything – of which the conception of the Hebrew *Abraham and Isaac* was meant to be proof, but which, in performance, utterly confounds its creator's artistic creed – is at the root of Hensher's dismissal of Britten's work. That Britten's music can profoundly move us is just too damned suspicious. The *War Requiem* moves us as a complete work of art, which is how music most often operates, through a conspiracy of its verbal and dramaturgical juxtapositions, its musical narrative, its existence as unmusical noise in certain places, and even the sheer look of it; its aesthetic is diverse, not musicologically abstract or doctrinally ruthless. It is, above all, human.

That humanity is something that Stravinsky perceived as sentimentality. 'Kleenex at the ready,' he declared, 'one goes from the critics to the music, knowing that if one should dare to disagree with "practically everyone", one will be made to feel as if one had failed to stand up for "God Save the Queen".'

This crotchety response to the overwhelming success of the *War Requiem* has, however, to be understood as more than insecurity, the master's fear of losing his powers in the face of the younger generation; and also as more than an aesthetic objection to 'expressive' music. At issue is the validity of a direct artistic confrontation with the horrors of the twentieth century.

Stravinsky had written the musical work, *The Rite of Spring*, that, more than any other, seems to express the savagery of twentieth-century conflict, an unbridled musical depiction of primitive blood sacrifice. This iconic masterpiece (originally entitled *The Great Sacrifice*) was premiered little over a year *before* the outbreak of the First World War. It has come to be seen, like Holst's 'Mars, Bringer of War', from *The Planets* suite (completed before August 1914) as a portent.

As if scared by what he had summoned into being, Stravinsky's style and musical philosophy underwent radical change after 1914. The war was not to be addressed directly; and Stravinsky's *Soldier's Tale*, written in its last year, is not an emotionally engaged contemporary manifesto, as one might expect from the title, but rather a quirky and detached modernist fairytale. The poised classicism of Stravinsky's later work, his adoption of a sort of formalism, and dogged insistence that music could not express anything but itself, were symptomatic of the retreat from Romanticism of any sort that the war had induced, a highbrow incarnation of Noël Coward, the Jazz Age and Bright Young Things. Goodbye to all that, in Robert Graves's phrase. In that sense, Britten's *War Requiem*, and all the brouhaha surrounding it, the 'Battle of Britten' as Stravinsky called it, must have seemed distastefully direct and, in its engagement with savagery, a return to the aesthetic of *The Rite of Spring*. In a diary entry in 1931, a student Britten wrote of a performance of the latter work – 'Sacre – bewildering and terrifying. I didn't really enjoy it, but I think it's incredibly marvellous & arresting.'

The Great War did not really touch Britten, except in a more general sense. He was too young (born in November 1913) to remember its course or its rigours, and his close family did not suffer the losses that afflicted so many others. He grew up as an artist, of course, in the period of post-war disillusionment, of irony and detachment, but three things served to mitigate this. First, and essentially, his self-confessed Romanticism as a composer. 'If I had been born in 1813 instead of 1913 I should have been a romantic,' he told Hans Keller in the late 1940s, 'primarily concerned to express my personality in music.' Secondly, and despite his progressive interests, his upbringing in a musical culture that was insulated from Continental modernism. And thirdly, his view of the artist's social responsibility, forged in the Auden circle in which he moved in the 1930s and allied to his long-standing and apparently visceral pacifism.

All of these currents feed into the *War Requiem*, which is a culmination in Britten's work and, rather like *The Rite of Spring* for Stravinsky, a stylistic turning point. It quite consciously works with register and style to achieve a synthesis between public statement and private questioning that is, formally, masterful. The sound and fury of the settings of the Latin mass text itself, with that Stravinskian rhythmic drive and Verdian theatricality, are set against chamber settings of war poetry by Wilfred Owen, which combine the instrumental and gestural economy of modernism with the interiority and sheer melody of the Romantic. The piece somehow symbolises reconciliation through the seamless interweaving of Germanic and non-Germanic conceptions of aesthetics, the metaphysical in concert with the human and contingent. For this was how the cultural aspect of the European civil war had manifested itself: a struggle, as the Germans had it, between *Kultur* and *Zivilisation*. The *War Requiem* seems to transcend all this, a hymn of healing as much as a manifesto of pacifism.

If Stravinsky was latching onto something about the *War Requiem* that he distrusted – that an occasional work decrying the European wars of the first half of the twenti-eth century was bound to be, in his terms if not ours, senti-mental – his scoffing at the popular acclaim it attracted was perceptive. For Britten himself was arguably unsettled by the scale of public success – his last opera, *Death in Venice*, is in part a study of an artist hollowed out by celebrity – and after the *War Requiem* he forged a more austere and less crowd-pleasing style.

Philip Hensher's view of the *War Requiem* as 'a terrible, literary sort of din' is worth returning to, as the modern incarnation of the Stravinskian discomfort. 'We all know', he wrote in the *Guardian*, 'what we think of the First World War: it's very sad. We all know what we think of Wilfred Owen's early death: it's very sad. And since the *War Requi-em* is about these two deeply moving things, it must, there-fore, be deeply moving itself, mustn't it?'

The *War Requiem* uses Owen's poetry for its own pur-poses, aesthetic and ideological (the poet-soldier Owen was no pacifist), but the piece is not in any sense *about* Owen. We are told nothing about him, although words from a projected preface to his poems do stand on the front page of the score as epigraph: 'My subject is War and the pity of

War. The Poetry is in the pity . . . All a poet can do today is warn.' Warning through pity; this is at odds with the Stravinskian aesthetic, dangerously personal, dangerously engaged. 'Some of my right-wing friends loathed it,' Britten is reported to have said, '"though the music is superb, of course," they'd say. But that's neither here nor there to me. The message is what counts.'

The *War Requiem* is, overtly, and perhaps surprisingly, about the First World War. 'The idea of the W.R. did come off I think,' Britten wrote to his sister, '. . . & how one thinks of that bloody 1914–18 war especially – I hope it'll make people think abit.' This is unexpected in a piece whose commission originated in the destruction of Coventry in 1940. Indeed Britten seems to veer away from addressing many of the experiences of the Second World War in his *Requiem*. He chose an English, a German and a Russian soloist as, in his own words, 'representatives of the three nations that had suffered most during the war'. This was a brilliant aesthetic gambit – the reconciliation of old enemies, English and German, presided over by the searing Russian soprano, embodying at times a cruel and somehow alien God, at times an unbearable weight of lamentation – but an odd sentiment to express in view of the Holocaust, Hiroshima and Nagasaki, or the invasion of Poland. Britten had responded darkly and savagely to his one direct experience of the horrors of war – his visit to Belsen with Yehudi Menuhin in 1945 – with a work, *The Holy Sonnets of John Donne* for voice and piano, much of which pulsates with guilt, sin and self-loathing. Britten's return to 1914–18 reflects both the immense significance of that war as the beginning of all the horrors of the twentieth century, and a catastrophe that musicians of the time had been unable adequately to address; but also, I think, the awkwardness and wariness of a pacifist who had experienced the Second World War, seen its horrors, but been present only as a bystander. Towards the end of his life, in the settings of two poems in English by the Scottish poet William Soutar that form part of the cycle *Who are these Children?*, Britten did, directly and powerfully, address the horrors of aerial bombardment directed against civilians in general, and children in particular.

In the end, as I have experienced it in performance, and despite Britten's apparent commitment to its pacifist 'message', the *War Requiem* is, I repeat, about far more than twentieth-century war and its horrors. It looks death in the face, and presents a terrifying vision of implacable holiness in, for example, the 'Sanctus'. The religion of humanity and the religion of the saints confront each other and achieve an ambiguous resolution.

Paul Kildea's *Selling Britten* offers a new approach to understanding the composer. It moves beyond musicological or even quasi-biographical analysis of the oeuvre to study the hard realities of markets and financial constraints. For a long time now, much work on Britten has been caught between the official line of the generation who were personally close to the composer, who 'bought into' the composer's own priorities; and those who reacted, sometimes bitchily, against the myth-making.

Yet analysis of the creation, structure and evolution of artistic myths need not involve denigration. Britten was a shrewd composer with a keen sense of his status and opportunities. Kildea shows how alert he was to the market constraints and opportunities of the 1930s, in terms of the genres in which he worked (choral pieces, occasional works, children's music) and the relationships he cultivated, particularly with the BBC, which emerges as a key cultural patron from its earliest years. It was this climate that made Britten a practical composer, and it was a practicality of which he was proud. The work with the GPO Film Unit (its most famous result, the Auden–Britten poem-documentary, was *Night Mail* of 1936), had an enormous influence on his efficiency as a composer writing to deadline. The idiosyncratic palette of instrumental colour particularly suited to film work was, as Kildea points out, transmitted to the chamber operas of the post-war period – *The Rape of Lucretia*, *Albert Herring*, *The Turn of the Screw* and the three church parables.

The irony is that Britten's commitment to a supposedly economical brand of opera has by no means encouraged his reception into the repertory. It is the expansive and expensive *Peter Grimes* (1945), whose eccentricities can be squeezed into the operatic straitjacket, that has entered the international repertory to become a staple of the big European and American houses. Since Jon Vickers's appropriation of the role, it has been a star vehicle for the *Heldentenor* and flourishes as a result. The fact that this is a million miles away from Britten's own taste and preoccupations is irrelevant; and this is as it should be, since the greatest musical works escape the limitations of their composer's intentions. But Britten's music-theatre masterpiece, *The Turn of the Screw* (1954), though frequently revived, remains problematic for larger houses and, alien as it is to the grand-opera tradition (a baker's dozen of players, six singers including two children, no chorus), has not become a repertory familiar in the same way as *Grimes*.

Kildea recognises that this problem existed from the start

for Britten and embodied a conflict between a developing infrastructure sponsored by the Arts Council and the demands of artistic freedom, both in terms of Britten's control of the whole creative process in opera, and his own aesthetic predilection for chamber sonorities and intimate communication. Covent Garden, the Council's preferred client, longed for native grand opera, but when Britten moved to supply it, his sensibilities were bruised. The terrible reception of *Gloriana* at its gala premiere in 1953 has become part of the Britten myth, the metropolitan act of philistinism which drove the composer into Suffolk isolation. While this is substantially true, an important part of the story has hitherto been neglected. It was Britten himself who insisted on a gala premiere ('Mr Britten would very much prefer the first performance to be given on the Gala night, because the opera was written as an offering to the Queen') in the presence of the monarch, against the very sensible misgivings of the Covent Garden board, who recognised that 'the kind of audience that one attracts on such an occasion is on the whole not the type one wants for a first performance'.

This episode shows us the typical Britten – managing his public persona, ambitious for recognition, but at the same time nervous of the outcome, suspicious of its fruits. The public failure of *Gloriana* meant retreat to the provinces; the overwhelming public success of the *War Requiem* was followed by the cryptic intimacy of much of the work of the mid- to late 1960s.

Many of the essays and interviews reprinted in *Britten on Music* manifest these paradoxes. The most substantial piece, Britten's famous lecture *On Receiving the First Aspen Award*, formulates most clearly his solution to the conflicting demands of artistic expression and public life, offering a vision of creative freedom expressed within a recognisably local community. Music should be occasional, written with particular performers in mind, constantly aware of the 'holy triangle' of composer, performer and listener.

Such practical constraints could liberate; 'to enter in these bonds is to be free,' as John Donne, one of Britten's favourite poets, has it. This ideology accounts for Britten's strange hostility to recording, for him in many ways such an educative force and such a means of dissemination (as Paul Kildea documents). Dislocated as it is, the gramophone cannot be 'part of true musical experience'.

When Britten was a child, his mother supposedly predicted his fate as the fourth of the great three Bs of classical music, Bach, Beethoven and Brahms. It is surely significant that he left behind his childhood enthusiasms for the Romantically heroic Beethoven or the internationally celebrated master Brahms, to make his exemplars Bach (working in barely appreciated isolation in Leipzig), and Schubert (writing so very substantially for his own circle). Of course, this was a sort of fantasy for the maestro of Aldeburgh, who could call a Rostropovich, a Richter or a Fischer-Dieskau to join in his *Hausmusik*, but it was a creative and necessary fiction.

This problematic mediation between the public and the private was crucial for Britten in so many facets of his career. It governed the rhythm of his oscillation between large-scale music and chamber works of all sorts; it informed his relationship with the critical community; but it was also embedded in the works themselves. The moral complexity of *Peter Grimes*, the difficulty of coming to terms with its anti-hero, surely reflects Britten's own ambivalence about

Peter's proxy status as repressed homosexual or embattled pacifist loner. *Billy Budd*, so clearly an opera about the conflict between personal feeling and public duty, contains a sexual subtext – Vere's and Claggart's very different desires for Billy – but also a Cold War allegory in which, as Robert Hewison has put it, 'the rules of war and the menace of revolution demand unbending conformity to public discipline, though at great personal cost'. This tension produced an extraordinary body of work to which those who belittle Britten's achievement would do well to attend more closely, ranging as it does across every genre, from extrovert piano concerto to solo cello suite, from grand operas to the most intimate of songs.

The songs are indeed Britten's most personal statement, if only because his lover, Peter Pears, sang most of them, something Graham Johnson is alert to in his rewarding lectures, 'Britten, Voice and Piano', first delivered at the Guildhall School of Music and Drama in 2001. How extraordinary it was, as Johnson underlines, for the two men to perform the *Seven Sonnets of Michelangelo*, love songs to and for Pears, in wartime London. In themselves, the generic span of the vocal works is remarkable, creating a body of orchestral song – the *Serenade* for tenor, horn and strings, *Les Illuminations* (has any French composer set Rimbaud to music?), *Our Hunting Fathers*, the *Nocturne* – to rival that of Mahler; and a series of piano-accompanied song-cycles that render Britten the true twentieth-century heir of Schubert, Schumann and Wolf. It is no accident that Britten and Pears performed these German songs regularly; or that *Winter Words* starts in the same key as *Winterreise*. Both are Biedermeier cycles, as Graham Johnson calls them, offering a nice genealogy of the strange tone of the Britten work, at once cosy and metaphysical.

It seems to me that Britten lavished much of his greatest music on his song-cycles – the settings of Donne, Pushkin, Michelangelo, Blake, Hölderlin and Hardy – and that they define much of his uniqueness as a twentieth-century composer. A British composer, steeped in English verse, he nevertheless steered away from the prosy literalness that afflicts much English song, and set other languages throughout his career; but at the same time, unlike Stravinsky, who was uninterested in art-song as a genre, he remained convinced that music was expressive, affective, intimately associated with words – their colour and rhythm – and at its core, profoundly, if magically, semantic. The battle of Britten was first fought in the 1940s around the issue of whether a conscientious objector could be a significant national musical voice; the 1950s saw Britten's pre-eminence jealously disputed; and the triumph of the *War Requiem* was followed by the relative eclipse of the late years, when Tippett's music was all the rage. It would seem a good moment, now, to end the hostilities and recognise, apart from anything else, Britten's special achievement as the only composer in the great tradition to have written a body of great operas *and* great songs.

2003

Britten's Letters

Review of *Letters from a Life: The Selected Letters of Benjamin Britten*, vol. 4 1952–1957, edited by Philip Reed, Mervyn Cooke and Donald Mitchell

'O dear, o dear, how I sometimes wish I were respectable & dead, & that people wouldn't get so cross.' Benjamin Britten is now dead (he would have been ninety-five this month), and, if the ubiquity of his music is a measure, highly respected if not quite respectable. Go to the Britten–Pears Foundation website and a calendar of performances shows several live performances of Britten works, large and small, every day of the year, all over the world. Most of his works have never been out of the recorded catalogue. Of the generation of classical composers who came to maturity in the wake of the Second World War, he is the flagship, the emblem, the victor. Yet, and in the face of music that is heartfelt, embedded in the great tradition, largely consonant, while at the same time avoiding kitsch or ironic reworking – in other words music with its own confident voice – he remains curiously unloved. Suspected for his supposedly pederastic leanings – an issue that John Bridcut has brilliantly reconfigured in his book and television documentary *Britten's Children*, recognising the desire not to abuse but rather to remain a child that lay at the heart of Britten's imagination – he is also presented as a twisted figure, with his 'corpses' (friends and associates who lost favour) and his fawning court.

A more empathetic understanding might see the difficulties involved in maintaining a virtually open homosexual marriage in the sexually repressive 1950s; might appreciate how fame and distinction both attracted and repelled a composer whose working motivation always had a puritanical edge. Loyalty was understandably important, and despite the feuds and petty unpleasantnesses of life in Britten's Aldeburgh milieu (the dismissal of the English Opera Group's General Manager Basil Douglas is conveyed here in all its nastiness by a brief sequence of letters), the composer evidently had both some self-knowledge as regards his capacity to wound, and a sense of guilt. During the tour of *The Rape of Lucretia* in the late 1940s, he recalled 'one very serious quarrel which I myself was involved with, with one of my closest friends in the company. And I can remember Kathleen [Ferrier] taking me aside one day and saying "Look, do try and be nice." And so I tried to be nice – and it worked.'

One thing that emerges in a casual way from this latest volume of letters is Britten's capacity both to be irritable, but also to apologise. Here he is, writing to Myfanwy Piper during the stressful period leading up to the completion of *The Turn of the Screw*, with the composer having both to write the music and worry about the financing of its English Opera Group premiere at La Fenice in Venice:

My dear Myfanwy, So sorry I was so short & sharp on the telephone this afternoon; only it's been a vile day, just on the edge of thunder, & work doesn't seem to come very easily, & figures on the top of everything is a bit much!

Britten's letters are full of such stuff. He himself recognised his limitations as a writer – 'Letters are so feeble, unless one is a writer, that it seems senseless to bother to put pen to paper.' Compared to Mozart's correspondence with his father, or the diaries of Prokofiev, Britten's letters are mostly unilluminating about the details of artistic creation, and flat in tone, astonishingly lacking in urbanity (Communist Yugoslavia is 'adorable – wonderful people, young enthusiastic, brave and musical'; Nehru 'a wonderful saintly man, yet gay as well') or literary interest. One feels a little cheated. This, after all, was a dedicated pacifist, a homosexual pioneer, a man who was central to the Auden circle in the 1930s, who worked with assurance in the setting of literary text in song, and in the dramatic construction of opera, with the unique achievement of a Shakespearean operatic masterpiece, *A Midsummer Night's Dream*, using the playwright's own words (roughly half the text of the play). Though Britten could display a remarkable literary sensitivity (who else could have set the dark knotty intensity of John Donne with such a stamp of authority?), his own literary skills were nugatory. The most extensive statement of his artistic creed, the elegant speech he made on receiving the Aspen Award, was reputedly put together by Pears. In the end, one of the hidden themes of this volume is Britten's escape from the literary lions with their more or less justified pretensions – Auden, Montagu Slater, Ronald Duncan, E. M. Forster – and his embrace of more serviceable, tractable librettists (William Plomer and Myfanwy Piper) who, in deferring to Britten's acute literary and theatrical instincts, produced much better structured work.

That doesn't mean that this latest volume isn't full of fascinating material, much of it to be found in the copious notes to the letters written by the editors, and the extensive reprinting of reviews of the works that dominated the period in question, the two operas, *Gloriana* and *The Turn of the Screw*, and the ballet *The Prince of the Pagodas*.

Gloriana was one of the 'great disasters of operatic history', as George Harewood described it in his memoirs. With a libretto by Plomer (in one of cultural history's more unexpected cross-currents, Plomer was the dedicatee of Ian Fleming's *Goldfinger*, with an enthusiasm for things Japanese reflected as much in Britten's later Noh-influenced *Curlew River*, for which Plomer wrote the libretto, as in the Bond thriller about a Japanese suicide garden, *You Only Live Twice*, which he edited), it was a deft interweaving of the public and private lives of Elizabeth I. It had plenty of scope for ceremonial, in a piece intended for Coronation celebrations at Covent Garden, but its main narrative focus was on a crisis of authority typical of much Britten opera (the Governess, Aschenbach, Captain Vere), centring on the ageing Queen's vexed relationship with her dashing Earl of Essex, drawing on Lytton Strachey and the more recent work of the historian J. E. Neale. Britten was clear from the outset: 'It's got to be serious. I don't want to do just folk dances and village green stuff.'

What emerges from the letters and their apparatus is the touching commitment of the new Elizabethans, Elizabeth II and her consort, to the project. They attended a dinner party organised by Harewood at which some of the music was sung round the piano, were appreciative and engaged, and prepared for the premiere to such an extent that Plomer claimed Prince Philip knew the libretto better than he did. What did for the opera's medium-term reputation was a premiere before a Covent Garden audience more great than good, and largely uninterested in music – 'an audience of stuck pigs', as the composer viciously dubbed them. They, and a large segment of the Establishment, resented the fact that Britten had not produced a *Merrie England* for its time. 'We all feel so kicked around, so bewildered by the venom, that it is difficult to maintain one's balance,' Britten wrote to one close friend in America. In the context of 1950s homophobia (it was around this time that Britten and Pears were allegedly being considered for criminal investigation by Scotland Yard), it is tempting to see moral panic at work, a desire for easier certainties than Britten, despite his co-option into British high society, was prepared to provide. More generally, Britten had shown from the outset, with *Peter Grimes*, that he was not interested in operatic cliché. As he wrote of *Gloriana*: 'Make [Essex] into the traditional hero, or his relations with the Queen more simple and direct, we cannot. This part of the story must always remain elusive, but to me always fascinating.' But if narrative simple-mindedness was to be eschewed, transparency of musical means was not:

[W]hat I'm pleased with, and what has got people down, is the simplicity and directness, the fewness of the notes. This has been confused with thinness of invention. Time will show if they are right about this, but from a point of view of attitude or technique I'm sure I'm right, for this work at any rate. There is also room in the world for *Lulu*.

The next opera, of course, *The Turn of the Screw* (which he was writing at the time he wrote this letter), was to be very much a homage to Berg's other, very different opera, *Wozzeck*.

A large section of the book is devoted to Britten's trip to the Far East, crucial to his development as a composer in providing a new set of musical practices which, while outside the norms of Western tonality, could be dissolved into it, avoiding the sort of arid avant-gardism that had come to dominate so much post-war composition. The first major result of this experimentation (though Britten had used gamelan sonorities before, in works such as *The Turn of the Screw*) was the full-length ballet score *The Prince of the Pagodas*. Working on this was the greatest struggle of Britten's professional life. 'That b. Ballet is FINISHED [double underlined], & I feel as if I've been just let out of prison after 18 months hard labour,' he wrote to his close friend Prince Ludwig of Hesse. It was an unprecedentedly long orchestral piece for the vocally inclined composer, and the arm's-length working pattern with the choreographer John Cranko was nothing like the hand-in-glove composer–librettist relationship he had grown used to. Also, Peter Pears, according to Britten's close associate Imogen Holst, was little interested in works in which he played no role, a painful absence no doubt (though how much Holst's own jealous possessiveness of Britten had to play in this view of Pears is not clear). In the end, *The Prince* has not become part of the Britten mainstream, but its idiom looked forward to another masterpiece, the last opera, *Death in Venice*, and back to the Russian tradition Britten so loved, and whose late twentieth-century inheritors (Shostakovich, Richter and Rostropovich) were so important to him from the 1960s on.

Dominated as the volume is by opera and ballet, it is important to notice the small masterpieces that were emerging in the interstices. *Canticle II* for two voices and piano, *Abraham and Isaac*, setting the text from the Chester Mystery Plays, was not only a precursor of *Noye's Fludde*, the children's opera from the same text, an analogue for the sacrificial relationship between Vere and Billy in the recently completed *Billy Budd*, and a source of musical material for the *War Requiem*; it also represented a real development in Britten's musical language, a new simplicity and greater resort to 'close motivic working' as the editors call it. It 'gave me great trouble in coming into the world', as he wrote in a letter. *Canticle III*, a setting of Edith Sitwell's 'Still Falls the Rain – The Raids, 1940, Night and Dawn', for voice, piano and horn, which he wrote after *The Turn of the Screw*, had a similar significance: 'I feel with this work & the Turn of the Screw . . . that I am on the threshold of a new musical world (for me, I am not pretentious about it!). I am worried by the problems which arise.'

It is fascinating to learn that the voice-and-piano cycle of Thomas Hardy settings, *Winter Words* (written in the wake of *Gloriana*), so convincingly cyclic in performance, emerged only gradually from a series of disparate songs. At the first performance they were announced simply as 'Hardy Songs', and it was Pears who suggested the title, which seems in retrospect to acknowledge Schubert's great winter cycle starting in the same key. One often senses with Britten that a lot was going on underneath, bubbling up and taking unexpected form, despite his supreme technical mastery. The composer's obsession in his works with dreams and the intertwining of imagination and the unconscious mind is significant here; it infuses the two English orchestral song-cycles, *Serenade* and *Nocturne*, *A Midsummer Night's Dream* and, of course, *The Turn of the Screw*.

A chamber-opera setting of Henry James's unsettling novella, this last is one of the acknowledged peaks of Britten's output, regularly revived despite its unconventional forces – thirteen instruments, four adults and two children. The ambiguity of dreams, the power of unacknowledged desires are at its core. It has always struck me that this opera, written in the same year as *Lord of the Flies*, plunges into the same sort of savagery of the child's unconscious as Golding's novel does, the jungle-drum rhythms of the Governess's journey to Bly a portent of what is to come.

What the letters reveal about the piece is how little the composer wanted to know what was going on as he wrote it, how little he was able to write words about the creative process; how much, when he did, he was either disingenuous or lacking in self-awareness. Here he is, discussing titles for the new opera with his librettist and only obliquely referring to the famous structural device by which the musical development of the opera, a series of variations, resembles the turning of a screw:

Thank you for your suggestions of titles. I do not feel that we have arrived yet, although something to do with 'Bly' is hopeful I think. I am not worrying about it at the moment until I am forced to, but I must confess I have a sneaking, horrid feeling that the original H. J. title describes the musical plan of the work exactly!!

One of the most terrifying moments in the whole opera, Act II, scene ii, when the children walk in like choirboys singing a sinister parodic Benedicite, is painted by Britten, in a letter to the director Basil Coleman, in the most innocuous light:

I feel so strongly, for the form & drama of the work as well as for the music's sake, that we must have something light and gay here, something for the children to be young & charming in (for the last time, almost, in the work) – & I think the idea of the hymn (a kind of 'choir procession') to be the best yet thought of.

Yet when the work was complete, Britten's sure-footedness as a musical dramatist, his conscious analytical mind, allowed him to express the heart of the matter in a way in which he had not allowed himself to do during actual composition: clear (as many confused critics of the opera are not) that on the issue of the reality or otherwise of the ghosts in the opera, 'Myfanwy Piper and I have left the same ambiguities as Henry James did'. Lacking in literary appeal, these letters are nevertheless an extraordinary testament to the interaction of conscious and unconscious strands in musical creativity, and to Britten's ability to keep the two in play.

2008

Britten's Song-Cycles for Orchestra

The great thing about Benjamin Britten's song-cycles with orchestra is that they exist at all. The orchestral repertoire for tenor is all too small. My first ideas of song with orchestra came from a well-worn LP of Jessye Norman singing Ravel's *Shéhérazade* and Berlioz's *Les Nuits d'été* with the London Symphony Orchestra under Sir Colin Davis. The former is clearly out of bounds for the male voice. The latter, arguably the first orchestral song-cycle, is something male singers can and should appropriate, even if the piece has been almost monopolised by sopranos and mezzo-sopranos. The poetic voice is male, and the songs were written originally for a varied clutch of singers, male and female. The influence of Berlioz is surely there, even if largely undocumented, in Britten's output, in the teenage assurance of the *Quatre Chansons Françaises* for orchestra and soprano, and later too. In the early 1970s, listening to Janet Baker singing the Berlioz cycle, Britten was eager 'to write you a piece like that'.

Mahler is the other colossus in this repertoire, something Britten obliquely reflected in his dedication of the *Nocturne* to the composer's wife, Alma. Merging the symphonic with the song, while at the same time employing the chamber orchestration that so influenced his British successor, Mahler created a great imposing mass of musical stuff – *Das Lied von der Erde*, *Lieder eines fahrenden Gesellen*, *Kindertotenlieder*, the *Rückert Lieder*, the settings of *Des Knaben Wunderhorn*. The mezzo and the baritone have the most opportunities in this repertoire, I selfishly observe. It was left to Britten, a precocious admirer of Mahler's music, to create for a tenor a similarly extraordinary body of work in this genre. Just as in opera, he created peerless dramatic and poetic opportunities for what was, in conventional terms, an unheroic voice: that of his life's companion, the tenor Peter Pears.

In some senses, of course, this was happenstance. If the protagonist of *Peter Grimes* was originally intended to be a baritone (like the role he was modelled on, Berg's Wozzeck), Britten's early works in the genre of orchestral song were written for the Swiss soprano Sophie Wyss. *Our Hunting Fathers*, his opus 8, written under the influence of W. H. Auden, has all the devastating energy and aggressive edge of the *enfant terrible*. That urge to shock is more successfully tamed and engaged in the other piece he wrote for Wyss, *Les Illuminations*. The choice of text is a surprising one. Rimbaud is not a poet whose work has been part of the French song tradition (the only other setting I can think of is Hans Werner Henze's *Being Beauteous*), and it may be that the quasi-musical sonorities of his language have discouraged native composers. Be that as it may, Britten's use of French functions as a sort of theatrical mask. The role-playing it permits opens up a realm of freedom and fantasy that expands into and beyond Rimbaud's linguistic virtuosity. Ferocity of invective is yoked with the humour of the *flâneur* and a melting sensuality of utterance, making *Les Illuminations* the great masterpiece of Britten's first period.

Britten's choice of Rimbaud is striking in so many ways: the overt homoeroticism; the identification with the predicament of the exile, Britten in (or close by) New York, Rimbaud in London, both cities evoked in 'Villes' in all their excitement and horror; and, closely connected, the not-at-all coincidental juxtaposition of an English musician setting French and a French poet refracting his phrases through the unfamiliar structures of the English language. *Les Illuminations*, prose poems, are full of snatches of English ('Being Beauteous' is one of many), but it is also notable that many of the strange turns of phrase in the French become clear if translated into English, the language in which Rimbaud was immersed (as immigrant and teacher) as he struggled to make sense of London's bizarre modernity. One often hears the complaint that Britten has somehow mangled the French language in setting *Les Illuminations*; in the face of Rimbaud's own strange melding together of French and English this seems an impertinent criticism of the composer. And the literary-cum-musical pun with which the piece opens is sublime in its perfectly controlled exuberance. 'Fanfare' is defined by a thrilling aural effect, an optical illusion for the ear, as string fanfares in B flat and E struggle for possession of an E/F trill. 'J'ai seul la clef de cette parade sauvage,' declares the singer as composer: I alone have the *key* of this savage parade (a melding of French and English again – the French word for musical key is *tonalité*).

Les Illuminations is a work of transition. Containing, in 'Being Beauteous', an erotic vision dedicated 'To P.N.L.P.' (Peter Pears), it was also the work that represented Britten's professional allegiance to his companion. 'Peter has shown people now how it really goes,' wrote Britten. Intended at the time for Sophie Wyss, it became a part of Pears's repertoire and Wyss disappeared from Britten's life, a relic of the Auden years. Musically, *Les Illuminations* is both the climax to the work of early mature Britten and the bridge between the overt radicalism of *Our Hunting Fathers* and the elegiac tone of the *Serenade* for tenor, horn and strings. *Les Illuminations* is full of a young man's anger, with a fizzing satirical edge that is missing from the later works, but it also says goodbye to all that in the song with which the composer chooses to close the cycle: 'Départ dans l'affection et le bruit neufs!' If the final rejection of bohemianism was delayed some months (and followed a stay in an extraordinary artists' commune in New York, frequented by Gypsy Rose Lee), 'Départ' nonetheless prefigured it. And, by giving Rimbaud's prose visions a shape which, as published, they do not have – a beginning, a middle and an end – Britten somehow gives rein to all this savagery and invective while at the same time, ultimately, taming it.

If he had been born a hundred years earlier, Britten claimed, he would have been writing Romantic music. The *Serenade*, despite Britten's diffidence ('not important stuff, but quite pleasant, I think'), is a thoroughly Romantic piece, phantasmagorical and death-laden, a quality underlined by the use of the horn, that iconic instrument for Romantic composers, conjuring up forest depths and an inexpressible longing. At the same time, play-acting again, and inspired by the singular virtuosity of the player for whom the *Serenade* was written, Dennis Brain, Britten presents the horn in an unparalleled variety of moods and characters. The witty baroque flourishes of 'Hymn' are quite effervescent, while in 'Nocturne' the horn is even addressed by the singer as a bugle. In the final poem, 'Sonnet', the horn is silent, but the cello harmonics played just after the word 'amen' are a ghostly reminder of it.

In performance the piece, at first sight no more than an anthology of favourite English poems, has all the dramatic assurance of a Schubert song-cycle, with a shrewd pattern-ing of tension and release, and a submerged sense of decay which manifests itself even at the outset, as the day grows old. The sense of foreboding intensifies, culminating in the horror of the 'Dirge', which finds such exquisite virtuosic unwinding in the 'Hymn'. The 'Sonnet', 'Sleep', reviews the whole procedure in microcosm, moving again from innocence to sin and back. But it is the brilliant touch of the horn prologue and epilogue that sets the seal on the master-piece. We hear it close up at the outset, distant at the close, and played with natural harmonics which conjure up a lost world of simplicity and natural order. The wordlessness of the procedure, before and after so many extraordinary words, both lends the whole piece an openness of intent – its meaning or emotional conclusion never pinned down – and somehow consecrates it as ritual. One might compare the repetitive drone of the hurdy-gurdy at the end of Schu-bert's *Winterreise* or, much more closely, the procession and recession of Britten's own *A Ceremony of Carols*, composed at much the same time.

The *Nocturne* is both akin to and very different from the earlier two cycles. *Les Illuminations* is for strings only; the *Serenade* for strings and horn. With a turn of the screw, the *Nocturne* is for strings and seven obligato (Britten's spell-ing) instruments that – soloists in each of the central seven movements – join forces only at the last. There is no pro-logue or epilogue, no fanfare or envoi; the piece melts into and out of existence. It is one of those works, like Britten's opera *A Midsummer Night's Dream*, written the following year, that emerges from nothingness, barely seeming to start at all, crystallising a music that has somehow hung in the air before the piece has even begun. In emotional contours, of course, the *Nocturne* is similar to the *Serenade*, with its central nightmare (unusually, here, a political one, Wordsworth's vision of Paris following the September Massacres, a masterful piece of suffocating claustrophobia in Britten's setting), a movement of virtuosic release (the Keats ditty for flute and clarinet that is preceded and thus deferred by the aching cor anglais lament of the Wilfred Owen setting), and an elegiac last movement, a Shakespeare sonnet.

It is this last setting that has always mystified me, its lush Romanticism so at odds with the spareness of a cycle that is self-consciously constructed out of fragments and marginal texts, bound together by the return between each song of the lulling breathing in the strings set up in the first song (a structural principle absent from Britten's previous cycles). The repeated descending motif of the last song is the solution to its mystery, borrowed as it is from one of Britten's favourite composers, Tchaikovsky, and in the same key as its source, the finale of the 'Pathétique' Symphony.

This last song of the *Nocturne* is often given a vague Mahlerian provenance, and interpreted as a straightforward love song for Pears. Love songs in Britten are never uncomplicated. The *Michelangelo Sonnets* for voice and piano had originated as an idea before Pears' appearance in the composer's life, during Britten's unconsummated obsession with Wulff Scherchen, which awkwardly overlapped with his relationship with the tenor. If 'Being Beauteous' is dedicated to one, the almost equally erotic 'Antique' from *Les Illuminations* was for the other. Britten's parting gift to Pears, his last opera, *Death in Venice*, written more than thirty years later, dealt with the subject of a world-famous artist marooned in Venice and obsessed with a beautiful young man. The choice of subject is notable, given that one of the most painful periods of Britten's time with Pears had been during rehearsals for the *The Turn of the Screw*, in 1954, during which Britten's infatuation with the Miles of that production, the teenage David Hemmings, had teetered on the edge of scandal.

Throughout Britten's partnership with Pears, his attraction to young men or boys had both inspired and unsettled him, and *Death in Venice* tried to address the inspirational forces at work, as well as the dangers, for the man and for his art. The same complex of emotions is at work at the end of the *Nocturne*, I would suggest. Tchaikovsky suffered similar feelings, and the homosexual scandals surrounding him have sometimes been associated with his possible suicide and with the supposed death embrace of the 'Pathétique'. What is certain is that he dedicated the symphony to his nephew, with whom he had been infatuated since the boy was eleven or twelve. The thematic basis of the last movement of the *Nocturne* is obviously related to Tchaikovsky's notion of his own last movement 'dying away': sleep and death are closely bound, a quite Shakespearean conceit. The rhetorical grandeur of Britten's score at this point, compared to the rest of the cycle, has clear practical roots in the scoring – chamber orchestra, rather than the strings plus soloist of the earlier movements – but it is used to convey something rather clotted; the overwhelming sense is of struggle, and at one point the vocal line almost breaks down ('when in dead night'). The quotation from Tchaikovsky points at an assimilation between his sexual struggles and Britten's.

Only at the very end of the song, as we return to the clearer texture of the opening of the whole piece, do we find the resolution that we might expect, and it is, indeed, one founded in a vision of sustaining love: 'All days are nights to see till I see thee, / And nights bright days when dreams do show thee me.'

2005

In the course of rehearsals for Death in Venice *in 2007 I started to notice another piece of Tchaikovskerie in Britten's music. If the end of the* Nocturne *quotes the last movement of the 'Pathétique', the opening of Act II of* Death in Venice *– the moment at which Aschenbach has to confront the reality of his feelings for the boy Tadzio; the moment also, just as significantly, at which his spiral into degradation and death begins – is bathed in the instrumental sonorities and the very same key as the dark opening to Tchaikovsky's last symphony. No coincidence, surely.*

Billy Budd

By presenting *Billy Budd* in a concert performance, we hope to allow the theatre of the imagination full rein by focusing on the music as drama for and of itself.

Billy Budd is cosmic not only because the forces involved are enormous – so different from the chamber orchestrations of many of Britten's other stage works – but also because it deals with the deepest issues of good and evil. Milton's narrative of the Fall was a palpable influence on the story as originally conceived by Hermann Melville. His novella, *Billy Budd, Sailor (An Inside Narrative)* is threaded through with religious imagery, as is Britten's opera.

At the same time, neither opera nor novella have the confident demeanour of religious certainty. Britten often picked his subjects for their ambiguity and troubling lack of clear definition, no more so than in *Billy Budd*. 'Truth uncompromisingly told will always have its ragged edges,' wrote Melville in the course of a narrative that, at his death, remained unfinished and in manuscript. And while the music may move us, it never compels us to a clear view of Captain Vere's dilemma, one that Britten placed at the centre of the opera: the conflict between social duty and personal morality.

The bare bones of the plot are easy to summarise: the monster of depravity, Claggart, master-at-arms of the *Indomitable*, plots to destroy Billy Budd, the young and handsome foretopman, only recently impressed. His motives are fathomless: he hates Billy, it seems, simply because he is good, handsome, unspoilt except for his tendency to stammer under stress; and, this being the time of the French Revolutionary wars, he invents a plot in which Billy has suborned his shipmates to mutiny with French gold. The *Indomitable*'s Captain, Edward Fairfax 'Starry' Vere, who has noticed Billy's qualities and distrusts Claggart, brings the two men together. Claggart accuses Billy of mutiny; Billy, unable to speak, strikes him dead. He is tried on board ship. Vere, despite himself, does not intervene in the judicial process. Billy is hanged. Each of us will come away from *Billy Budd* with a different view of Vere and his inability or refusal to save Billy; the same is true in relation to the Governess in *The Turn of the Screw*, another singularly ambiguous text turned into an opera by Britten.

The inability to speak out is a dramatic conundrum Britten uses more than once. The second act of *Death in Venice*, is partly, if ambiguously, driven by the writer Gustav von Aschenbach's mute self-consciousness in relation to Tadzio which disables him from being able to warn the boy's family about the spreading cholera epidemic. He remains trapped within himself. In *The Turn of the Screw*, the Governess is unable to write to the uncle who has commissioned her to take care of the children at Bly. Even in *Peter Grimes*, the apprentice boy's inability to speak – his scream as he falls from Peter's hut is his sole utterance – is surely of some significance.

In *Billy Budd* we have two mirroring instances of speechlessness: Billy's physical incapacity, to refute Claggart, due to his stutter, which the prelude to the opera establishes as a metaphor for the imperfection of God's supposedly harmonious creation; and Vere's incapacity, his willed refusal (or is it a disciplined denial?) of Billy's plea for intervention and mercy at his trial.

It is Britten's greatness to dazzle us with the enormous canvas of *Billy Budd*, to stir us and move us but, at the end, to leave us troubled and unsettled: to compel us to examine the story we have been told and question our own deepest convictions.

2007

I wrote this brief note to introduce a concert performance of the opera at the Barbican, with the London Symphony Orchestra under Daniel Harding. Having been given the marvellous opportunity to programme a series of concerts at the hall over a residency of two seasons, Billy Budd *was an obvious choice: an opera that I longed to be part of but which had not yet come my way in the ins and outs of operatic planning. In fact, I had been asked to sing Vere in a new production in Munich some years before, but the decision had been made to perform the original four-act version which Britten had withdrawn in favour of the two-act revision. I harboured the same reservations about the so-called muster scene at the end of the original Act II that Pears and, in due course, Britten had felt. This, in the four-act version, is our introduction to Vere. It means that we see him first (prologue aside) as a man of action. But it is a scene with which Britten was unhappy – too heroic for Pears, too Gilbert-and-Sullivan for the critics, and, I would argue, untrue to Melville's conception of Vere. I felt unable convincingly to sing it, so I reluctantly withdrew.*

I was a little nervous about our Barbican performance, both about mounting a concert performance of a profoundly theatrical work, and also because it would be the first time I would confront the role of Captain Vere. What is more, we were to record the performances for a future CD release. In practice, the idea of the theatre of the imagination can and did work. Billy

Budd *benefits from a degree of musical concentration on the part of the audience which may be missing in the opera house. A certain metaphysical poetry, a symphonic level of abstraction, is released which the literal representation of details of maritime life can inhibit. And I tried to use some of the methods I had discovered in the theatre to bring the role alive. I see this as a matter of engaging with the text of the opera itself – seeing how the music and the libretto pull together, and sometimes apart – but also looking outside for hints and suggestions. For me, building a role is about taking all these fragments into oneself, into a sort of melting-pot; and allowing one's own personality and predispositions, both as a human being and more specifically as a performer, to act as a magnet drawing everything into its field of force and making sense of it. It is not as if there is a 'character' called Captain Vere who can be 'discovered' by close attention to the score. The performance that the audience receives is made out of the coalescence of the score and the performers with all their particularities.*

Working with the director Deborah Warner on The Turn of the Screw *for the Royal Opera back in 1997, we found the Henry James novella enormously useful as a psychological guide, and also as a source of stage directions – above all, as I remember, for the quality of looks between the protagonists. In the end, the production revealed to me Britten's extraordinary engagement with the text, and his absorption in and solution of the supposed problem of staging an ambiguous ghost story. The opera remains as troubling and ambiguous as the story, the physical manifestation of the ghosts notwithstanding.*

Another novella, Melville's Billy Budd, *can equally well be used to supplement the material directly presented in the opera. When Claggart first approaches Vere in order to accuse Billy, he provokes in him, even before the accusation is broached, 'a vaguely repellent distaste': 'a sort of impatience lurked in the intonation of the opening word . . . "Well? What is it, Master-at-arms,"' – words directly set in the opera. With 'a marked leaning toward everything intellectual', Vere is held by some of his fellow officers to be 'a dry and bookish gentleman . . . lacking in the companionable quality'. 'Between you and me now,' declares one, 'don't you think there is a queer streak of the pedantic running through him?' 'An unobtrusiveness of demeanour', Melville writes, 'may have proceeded from a certain unaffected modesty of manhood.' While we see Vere only on board ship, it seems interesting to me that we are told that 'ashore, in the garb of a civilian, scarce anyone would have taken him for a sailor'.*

Most striking of all is the sense at the end of the novella that Vere's behaviour is half-crazed, something unexpressed in the libretto but easily to be found in the music. The ship's 'prudent' surgeon, Melville tells us, unsettled by Vere's notion of trying Billy summarily on ship rather than seeking the authority of the admiral, 'recalled the unwonted agitation of Captain Vere and his excited exclamations, so at variance with his normal manner. Was he unhinged?' As so often in Britten's work, what is buried in the music goes well beyond the literal setting of the libretto. His reading of his sources infused his musical dramaturgy, often unconsciously.

Death in Venice

Most of us come to *Death in Venice* with preconceptions. The novella by Thomas Mann is one of the most celebrated texts in German literature and, for English speakers, the work of Mann's we are most likely to have read. But our view of it is likely to be refracted through the medium of that most art-house of all art-house movies, Visconti's *Death in Venice*, released in 1971.

On the eve of playing the lead in English National Opera's new production of Benjamin Britten's opera of the story, I still haven't seen the film – Britten, writing his opera at the same time as the film came out, was advised not to by lawyers anxious about plagiarism, an anxiety that I, as a performer, share. But images of an oddly mousy Dirk Bogarde as the besotted Aschenbach and Björn Andrésen as Tadzio, the sailor-suited adolescent object of his affections, have become part of the wider culture; Visconti's Tadzio was even used for the cover of Germaine Greer's 2003 hymn to youthful male beauty, *The Boy*. The film, however, had one musical side-effect: it brought Mahler to an unprecedentedly wide audience, inspiring one Hollywood mogul to the legendary rasp, 'Great score – who's this Mahler guy's agent?'

My disabling preconception about *Death in Venice* was over the age of the central character. Asked three or four years ago, before my fortieth birthday, if I would consider playing Aschenbach, I thought the idea ill-advised. The opera is associated with old age, through the circumstances both of its composition – Britten wrote it while suffering from the heart condition that was soon to kill him – and of its early performances, with a sixty-two-year-old Peter Pears as Aschenbach.

But looking at the novella again heartened me a little. Gustav Aschenbach was honoured with the aristocratic particle 'von' at the age of fifty, Mann tells us on page one, and according to his working notes, the distinguished writer is fifty-three. I am now forty-two and the distance seems no longer insurmountable (as anyone of forty-two will tell you). Moreover, the autobiographical content of *Death in Venice* is well known, and Mann was in his mid-thirties when he wrote it.

The outline of *Death in Venice* is simple and familiar. Suffering some sort of creative block, Gustav von Aschenbach resolves to travel to restore his faculties and, perhaps, find new inspiration. His journey to Venice and his stay there on the Lido are marked by unsettling incidents that seem to portend death and humiliation. His attention is seized by a beautiful young Polish boy, Tadzio, who has come, with his family, to the Hotel des Bains. Aschenbach's initial detached and aesthetic interest becomes a consuming obsession raging against the background of a cholera epidemic in the city. He finds himself unable to speak to the boy or to his family, even to warn them about the dangers in the city (which the authorities are trying to conceal). As the Polish family packs up to leave, Aschenbach sits on a virtually empty beach watching the boy walk out to sea, and dies.

Like Aschenbach, a creatively blocked Thomas Mann travelled to Venice in 1911 with his family. Almost all of the events described in the novella actually happened to him: the encounter with a mysterious traveller in a Munich graveyard that inspires the trip; the sighting of an elderly fop on board ship; the engagement of a truculent gondolier on the way to the hotel; the appearance of a fascinating Polish boy; and the advent of cholera (the last European outbreak, in fact). Out of these materials Mann wove a highly complex fable about fame and humiliation, the compromised dignity of the artist, the temptations and necessity of beauty, the dangers of repression and, conversely, the danger of letting go. During the 1930s, Mann himself even saw the book as a prophecy of Germany's degrading relationship with the Nazis.

Mann's *Death in Venice* is as suggestive and impossible to pin down as a piece of music. It is, at one and the same time, psychologically compelling and pulsating with symbolism. It is nineteenth-century realism projected on to a mythical plane. Despite the solipsistic nature of its protagonist, which Britten dealt with in a series of Aschenbach recitatives, it is – as Myfanwy Piper recognised when condensing it into an opera – highly theatrical in its construction. As with *Billy Budd* and *The Turn of the Screw*, Britten chose a complex and ambiguous story whose potential to suggest and unsettle is only enhanced by musical treatment.

One thing has become clear to me, and needs emphasising in view of contemporary preoccupations: neither the book nor the opera is about a paedophile – for that, you need to look at Nabokov's *Lolita*, a highly wrought literary artefact that cries out not to be made into an opera (or a film). Yes, Britten was notoriously attracted to adolescent boys; they inspired him, interested him and, as John Bridcut has suggested, he partly thought of himself as a thirteen-year-old. This is a curious thought but then, as Aschenbach says in the opera, 'Who really understands the workings of the creative mind?' However, it's equally clear that for all the interest and anxiety, nothing much happened; Britten was not an abuser. The late David Hemmings, object of that almighty crush during the creation of *The Turn of the Screw* in Venice in 1954, resolutely cleared him of any wrongdoing.

Thomas Mann's choice of Greek love – the love of an older man for a beautiful adolescent – for his novella was undoubtedly inspired by his own sexuality and by his own sighting of a Tadzio figure on the Lido. But that choice was also, more importantly, an aesthetic one, infiltrating an increasingly dominant Platonic and Socratic theme into the work, something Mann's original idea of a story about the elderly Goethe's passion for a teenage girl could not have done. Britten was obviously, in turn, drawn to the book by its homosexual theme; a beloved boy in Venice, of all places, was a piquant coincidence. But other themes gripped him too, notably the difficult relationship between self-discipline and creative fire that afflicted him in the early 1970s. The enormous popular success of the *War Requiem*, first performed in 1962, had unsettled him almost as much as the failure of the opera *Owen Wingrave*, which premiered in May 1971. His style was entering a new, more austere phase, and he felt himself to be unfashionable in the face of his friend and rival Michael Tippett. The issues of formalism in art and the perilous dignity of the acclaimed artist are central to *Death in Venice*.

The new opera was well received by the critics when it opened in 1973, but it has not achieved the popular success of *Peter Grimes* or *Billy Budd*. Instead, the work has been trivialised and misunderstood all the way along from Joan Cross (the first Ellen Orford in *Peter Grimes*), who talked of it as a work of homosexual propaganda 'preaching to the converted', to Kent County Council, which banned a production for schools in 1989, reportedly over worries that it promoted homosexuality, contrary to section 28 of the Local Government Act. This seems a weird judgement on a work in which a writer who admires a beautiful boy from afar on a Venetian beach is condemned to die of cholera. But if Britten's interest in the story was in some senses self-lacerating, revisiting distressing old scenes of impossible love, the work itself stretches much further.

I came to it knowing that the music alone – in its brilliant sound-worlds, its compelling musico-dramatic use of endlessly varied and reconfigured thematic material, its melodic invention – made Britten's *Death in Venice* perhaps his greatest opera. Preconceptions made me anxious about the story itself, but rehearsing it as a piece of theatre, we have found a gentleness, a sadness and a subtlety that belie the sensationalism that has too often afflicted the reception of this masterpiece. Britten's *Death in Venice* speaks of the human condition with a depth of insight few operas can match.

2007

Alex Ross: *The Rest is Noise*

Alex Ross's *The Rest is Noise* tells the story of what happened to Western classical music in the twentieth century. We all know that the invention of recorded sound around 1900 made possible an extraordinary dissemination of the riches of the classical repertoire – composed largely for the rich and powerful – to the mass of ordinary people. On the gramophone, the radio, television and, subliminally and hence more powerfully, through the movies, the classical sound in all its variants (even the supposedly rebarbative confections of the Second Viennese School) has insinuated itself into the culture at large. Never before have so many people listened to, or liked, so-called classical music. Yet this extraordinary triumph has culminated in a malaise: a feeling, widespread in the musical profession and elsewhere, that classical music is in crisis and that things have never been so bad. Classical music feels abandoned, left behind as history has moved on, sulking in its tent as the real cultural action happens somewhere else.

Ross's book – which, in a two-pronged attack, puts the history back into music and music back into history – offers many answers to this paradox. In a book packed full of well-chosen and depicted vignettes and anecdotes, two stand out.

In 1904, Richard Strauss, the 'anarch of art' as one American critic described him, visited the United States. He was received at the White House by President Theodore Roosevelt. He was invited on to the floor of the Senate.

How comforting this is for us besieged elitists, who grasp at such contemporary straws as the opera-loving Gordon Brown succeeding the Fender Stratocaster-wielding Blair. Once upon a time, serious music was given its due. Music does of course still have a political platform, a bully pulpit even; but it is pop musicians now who are wooed by political leaders, and classical musicians, with a very few exceptions (Daniel Barenboim springs to mind), who inhabit the margins. Whether political leverage, or cultural influence, were really good for classical music – tempting as it is to want to see the best of art appreciated and deferred to – is another question.

Thirty-eight years after Strauss's American apotheosis (and some years after his shameful but complex accommodation with the Nazi regime in Germany, masterfully unpicked by Ross), in the midst of the Great Patriotic War, the score of Dmitri Shostakovich's Seventh Symphony, the 'Leningrad', was flown into that besieged city by Soviet military aircraft. Musicians were recalled from more straightforwardly martial duties on the front line to perform it. German commanders planning to disrupt the performance found themselves pre-empted by 'Operation Squall', a Soviet diversionary manoeuvre. The symphony was relayed over loudspeakers into no-man's-land. As Ross puts it, 'Never in history had a musical composition entered the thick of battle in quite this way: the symphony became a tactical strike against German morale.'

If we were to ask why, at the opening of the twentieth century, and through the horrors of its first five decades, classical music retained such importance, the answer would have to be: Germany. Classical music – music that was more than entertainment, music that demanded reverent attention, and which even made metaphysical claims – was written into the very DNA of German culture. The German question, the political and diplomatic issue of how the German nation fitted into the world, dominated international affairs in the century between the 1848 revolutions and the Second World War. This was reflected in the philosophical and cultural preoccupations of the European elites, rooted as they were in German philosophical conceits and German political anxieties. Hegelianism, Marxism, nationalism, Wagnerism – love them or hate them, they all came from Germany and they framed the terms of debate in philosophy, political theory and music. If Schopenhauer put music at the centre of his philosophy as the most important art, one that uniquely traced the movements of the noumenal will, Wagner responded with music that fascinated and horrified artists in all disciplines. When it came to the great contest of the 1914–18 war, German propagandists such as Thomas Mann characterised it as a conflict between the *Kultur* of Germans and the *Zivilisation* of their French-led opponents; between, in musical terms, the deep, metaphysical character of the German tradition, and the superficial *joie de vivre* of the French.

The price paid for classical music's proximity to power was heavy, and the central chapters of Ross's book lay bare the moral somersaults composers turned, the degradation into which they sank. The cultural theory that the totalitarian regimes of the twentieth century had inherited from the nineteenth gave artists a dangerous potency, the all-too-useful capacity to become, in Stalin's words, 'engineers of human souls'. Stalin's amateur interest in classical music – he reputedly owned ninety-three opera recordings, nerdily writing critical remarks on his record sleeves – did nothing to protect composers such as Prokofiev and Shostakovich from the cultural policy of a regime that saw no role for anything that smacked of autonomous art. Shostakovich's output veered between the cryptic privacy of his chamber music, the crassness of his patriotic cantatas and songs, and the still-contested 'irony' of the major public works. Ross's analysis of the possibility of irony in music is at one and the same time sceptical and appreciative. 'To talk about musical irony,' he writes, 'we first have to agree what the music appears to be saying, and then we have to agree on what the music is really saying. This is invariably difficult to do.' His concluding advice is that one should 'stay alert to multiple levels of meaning', making Shostakovich's symphonies, the Fifth or even the supposedly propagandistic Seventh, 'rich experience[s]'. The consequence of Ross's superbly nuanced historical accounts of both Prokofiev's and Shostakovich's music is to send one back to the music with new ears.

In any aspirant totalitarian regime, cultural producers like musicians have to be overseen, goaded, persecuted and petted. Hitler's Germany was different only in that a musical vision of politics was uniquely central to the nightmare that was played out in the Reich between 1933 and 1945. It wasn't that music was too important not to be politicised, more that politics was music in another form: 'Politics aspired to the condition of music, not vice versa,' as Ross puts it. The threatening rhetoric of Hitler's coded language about the Jews from the Kroll Opera speech of 1939 on the eve of war, and the speeches from the period of the exterminations themselves, are drenched in Wagner, and Ross acutely picks out the references to *Parsifal* in the Führer's tirades. Hitler's very rise to power, his acquisition of the respectability that eased his accession, were helped by the musical culture he shared with the Wagner clan, which supported him from the early 1920s on, and whose fads and tastes – vegetarianism, animal rights, dabbling in Eastern mysticism – he enthusiastically adopted.

For Ross, the Nazi infatuation with music is the crux of his story. If nineteenth-century German politics and philosophy and musical endeavour made classical music unprecedentedly momentous, its implication in the near-annihilation of European civilisation by the mid-century robbed it of moral authority, a collapse with which classical music still lives, sixty years on. As Ross points out, trivially but accurately, 'When any self-respecting Hollywood arch-criminal sets out to enslave mankind, he listens to a little classical music to get in the mood.'

It is Ross's dissection of the career of Richard Strauss that most tellingly encapsulates classical music's twentieth-century tragedy. The book opens with the Graz premiere of *Salome* in 1906 (it had had its very first performance earlier the previous year in Dresden), conducted by the composer, and attended by Puccini, Schoenberg, Berg, Zemlinsky and Johann Strauss's widow – and also, very probably, by a little-known Austrian teenager called Adolf Hitler. By the mid-1930s, Strauss is enthusiastically hailing the new regime: 'Thank God, finally a Reich Chancellor who is interested in art!' By 1942, he is, at once brave and pathetic, demanding entrance atTheresienstadt – 'I am the composer Richard Strauss' – to try and rescue his Jewish daughter-in-law's grandmother. By 1945, he is writing the profoundly disillusioned *Metamorphosen* and trying to trade on his American fame – 'I am the composer of *Rosenkavalier* and *Salome*' – to gain preferential treatment from the occupying American forces. As with Shostakovich, the moral and historical complexities lead one back to the music.

Ross's broad historical argument, and his moral tale about music and power, occupy the central chapters of the book and inform much of the rest of it. His engagement with Stravinsky, Berg, Schoenberg, Sibelius and Britten is infectious; his accounts of New Deal arts policy, US Army sponsorship of Darmstadt modernism and 1960s inter-actions between art and pop music are revelatory. As for the music itself, Alex Ross's brave avoidance of musical notation and brilliant use of metaphorical and descriptive language mean that *The Rest is Noise* grapples with the actual stuff of music as few other books have done. And if you want to hear the sounds themselves, you can always go to his website at www.therestisnoise.com and listen.

2008

Bob Dylan

A lot of pop music lasts as pure nostalgia, summoning up an era in history or a time in our lives. Friends. Food. Sea. Sunshine. Dancing. Open windows into the garden, or the closed doors of sweaty dark basements. People talk about the soundtrack to their lives, and they usually mean pop music. We play it in our cars and we make of our journeys some sort of private *cinéma verité*, choreographing the unintended. In that respect, pop music is mood music. Bob Dylan's records are more than that. He shows that you can have the highest aspirations for popular music, in terms both of his own performance and of the sophisticated, multi-layered lyric. Dylan's music deserves attention and deepens our experience.

There have been many great singers of popular music who didn't have great voices. Fred Astaire had a weak voice, but was a great singer: Irving Berlin preferred him singing his songs to anyone else. The Dylan case is even more extreme. He has a rasping, often an unpleasant voice. But his ability to bend and stretch the melody in a very expressive way, while not seeming to pay overmuch attention to it, is extremely persuasive, almost despite itself. He shows us how performance, a fleeting art, can lift material. Musically, there's often little of interest, but he does things that, though you wouldn't necessarily want to hear anyone else do them, work for him. Often he'll be delivering a very simple melody, but he'll weave around it with his rough-edged non-voice, and somehow he makes it so that it's as if the words are gently moulding the melody. I find that both incredibly subtle and impossibly hard to imitate.

The perfect example of that is my favourite Dylan track, 'Don't Think Twice, It's Alright', on *The Freewheelin' Bob Dylan*. I don't know how planned it was: it seems very improvised, or at least improvisatory, when compared to the infinite care apparent in every tiny detail of a Frank Sinatra recording. There is surely a high degree of perfectionism at work in Dylan's efforts to sound casual, but never a sense of him being in any way a technical singer – although, like so many great popular singers, you don't feel that he is ever singing out of tune (even if he isn't singing exactly *in* tune either). If you detach ownership of his lyrics from Dylan (and the provenance of many of the tunes and arrangements he uses is unclear, as the Dylanologists will tell you), just his ability to use words as a communicator, to declare exclusive ownership of a song, is quite remarkable, and without peer in popular music.

As a writer of lyrics, as a performer, and as a consummate musician in the only sense that matters – moving us, making us think, challenging our notions and our nostrums – Dylan is at the very top. Questions about dumbing down or cultural relativism – the old BBC *Late Show* debate, 'Is Dylan better than Keats?' – are beside the point.

Dylan mixed folk, blues and country idioms in a way that was new; he was deeply influenced by the music-theatre tradition of Brecht, Weill and Lenya. The interpenetration of genres, the willingness to experiment, is a feature of most of the greatest music in the classical tradition. Schubert often uses a folk-ish, *Völkisch* idiom and folk colours, and that was one part of the excitement of music in that period.

Dylan also made pop musicians ambitious about lyrics,

influencing the Beatles into producing lyrics that aimed
to be as suggestive and polyvalent as his own. A song like
'Norwegian Wood' is obviously Dylan-influenced. And
even those songs of his own that are very specifically tied
to their time, like the Cuban Missile Crisis-era apocalyp-
tic vision, 'A Hard Rain's Gonna Fall' (again on *The Freewheelin' Bob Dylan*), are so full of extraordinary and pulsating imagery that they are not simply 'historical pieces' (I
first heard the track on a bus to a CND rally in the 1980s),
but still live as poetry and music in the highest sense. They
retain the power to communicate with the same integrity
and emotional directness.

Classical singers could definitely learn from Dylan in
terms of using different, unexpected, colours in their voices
to communicate the burden of a song. More importantly,
he demonstrates that in singing, the voice isn't really what
matters, it's what you do with it.

I remember the very first time I laid claim to Dylan – as
opposed to overhearing songs or listening to bits of other
people's LPs. I was sharing a study bedroom at boarding
school, aged about fifteen or sixteen, and I had been down
to the old HMV shop on Oxford Street to buy a copy of
Highway 61 Revisited. There were two or three big pivoting
windows with stand-on window sills overlooking Little
Dean's Yard, itself overlooked by the vastness of the Victoria Tower, the vast ceremonial entrance to the Houses of
Parliament, and Westminster Abbey, with its own fantastical Hawksmoor towers at the West End. I opened the windows wide and I switched on my record player full blast
and was completely transfixed by the daring of the opening track with that extraordinary whoop of a whistle, as
God asks an incredulous Abraham to kill his son. Where?

On Highway 61. It's a long way from the Abbey precincts, the road from New Orleans to the Canadian border, passing through Bob Dylan/Robert Zimmerman's birthplace in Duluth, Minnesota. This is the landscape of the blues, so much so that the 61 was known as 'the blues highway'. The song is a miracle of casual cultural reference. There's something extraordinary and moving, not simply pretentious, in being able to connect this song to a high medieval carving in Modena Cathedral, Britten's *Canticle II* and Kierkegaard's musings on the terrible inscrutability of the divine, all of them treatments of the literally awe-ful tale of Abraham and Isaac.

2003/2010

Hans Werner Henze

I first met Hans Werner Henze in 1996. We were celebrating his seventieth birthday at the Aldeburgh Festival and I had been asked to sing, with Julius Drake at the piano, his three song settings of W. H. Auden written in the 1970s: a simple elegy for a cat; a jagged evocation of Rimbaud; and a wonderful, sublime love song, a setting of one of the poet's most famous lyrics, 'Lay your sleeping head, my love, human on my faithless arm'.

Until then my views of Henze had been based on total ignorance – a glimpse of an atypically austere photograph, a notion that contemporary music was somehow forbidding. What I found in Henze's music, I found in him as a person as well – warmth and charm, a wit and a human sympathy he has shared with me and my family.

The other gift he was to give me was a song-cycle which, having heard me sing in Snape, he promised to write. Later that year he came to hear me sing Schumann's *Dichterliebe* at the Wigmore Hall (saying he didn't know the piece – mischievously perhaps?), and he listened to records of mine to familiarise himself with what I could do. I'd been a full-time singer for only a year, inspired to sing by one of the early performers of Henze's music, Dietrich Fischer-Dieskau, and immersed in the work of Benjamin Britten, who had also been an early Henze champion.

The idea of this canonical figure writing for me could have been intimidating, but Henze's laughter and flexibility, his lack of pomposity or grandeur about his own music-making, all quickly dispelled any such notions. His original intention was to set some poems by his friend the late Ingeborg Bachmann, the *Anrufung des Großen Bären*, returning to an idea he'd had for a cycle for Fischer-Dieskau in the 1950s. Instead, he turned to writing the poems himself, creating a mythic landscape based on his own trips to the Kenyan island of Lamu. Some of the characters in the poems are based on real people.

I particularly remember Henze's story of the boat that Fausto, his partner, gave him for his birthday, captained by the reckless Selim. The first song in the cycle *Sechs Gesänge aus dem Arabischen* is Selim's poetic and musical come-uppance. The last song is a setting of an invocation to the moon by Hāfiz, translated by Rückert – the only poem in the cycle not by Henze. I see in that a sort of letting-go, and the song itself has an extraordinary air of transcendence.

The cycle, although small-scale in terms of forces, feels monumental. Planned at thirty-five minutes, it actually lasts fifty: Henze said he had a defective metronome in hospital where he was finishing it.

Performing *Sechs Gesänge* at Hans's and Fausto's home in Marino, outside Rome, will always stick in my mind. As we reached the song about the moon, there indeed was the full moon, shining above the Roman countryside. A few years later at a birthday party in London, we performed the song again, alongside some Schubert and some English folk-songs. Afterwards, many people with no special interest in classical music, or any experience of so-called contemporary music, came up to say how much they had loved that particular song.

The cultural references in the *Sechs Gesänge* are various – a quotation from Goethe (the witch scene on the Brocken from *Faust*, a sort of in-joke on my academic research as a historian on witchcraft); a dedication to Giacometti for the praying mantis song; a song set in a cave where the Ebola virus has its mythic origin; echoes of Cavafy in 'Cäsarion'. So are the musical textures, from the transparent flute music of 'Cäsarion' to the quasi-orchestral grandeur and thickness of 'Ein Sonnenaufgang'.

My overwhelming feeling on performing the cycle – and Julius Drake and I must have given it some twenty times – is how it works on an audience. It's theatrical in the best sense; despite the moments of complexity and unfamiliarity, a non-specialist audience can be moved and challenged by the work, and see its transparent beauties and more resistant passages as part of a dramatic structure. This, for me, is Henze's great achievement: to write music that is modern, but acknowledges and is rooted in the past, that can be taken on board by an audience without resorting to mere superficial texture, simplification or kitsch.

For Henze, music is drama, and what matters is the overall effect, not the realisation of every pitch or rhythm on the page. Fidelity to the text is always important in the classical tradition, but living performance is an even more urgent necessity. In rehearsal he often asked for less voice, more speaking, not worrying about the notes.

He referred to some of the piano writing (much of it furiously difficult) as the representation of natural phenomena rather than written music. At one point, he said that the notes were not interesting enough to be heard properly. By this he meant, I think, that the effect of the music on its listeners, and indeed performers, has precedence over its literal construction.

Like Brahms, Britten or Schubert before him, Henze is prepared to let go of the music once it has been composed. In fact, he demands that the performer take hold of it and run. Despite the radicalism of much of his output, he is a Romantic, writing emotionally laden music – even though he is writing in an era when the Romantic creative impulse is deeply problematic, too often seen as insufficiently rigorous or in thrall to sentimentality. Much as he admired and learnt from Stravinsky, Henze could never have pretended that music did not express or crystallise feelings.

An early participant in the radical musical workshops held at Darmstadt in the 1950s, with other iconic figures such as Boulez and Stockhausen, he soon rebelled against their forbidding strictures. When future generations come to write the history of post-war music, I've no doubt they will see Henze's divorce from Darmstadt shibboleths, his forthright rejection of the pronunciamentos of the avant-garde, as a watershed. I like to think that the *Sechs Gesänge* marked a new phase for the composer. His next opera, *L'Upupa and the Triumph of Filial Love*, was on an Arabian theme to a libretto of his own. His literary gift and intelligent, critical mind have often been remarked upon; he speaks, and writes, a most beautiful and graceful English.

At the moment my mind is full of Henze's music because I've performed – in Berlin and Aldeburgh – a piece he wrote for Peter Pears: *Kammermusik 1958*, settings of Hölderlin for voice, guitar and chamber ensemble. I have cursed him (light-heartedly) because some of it is so difficult to learn; and blessed him for its manifold and extraordinary beauties. One of the movements asks 'Gibt es auf Erden ein Maß?' (Is there a measure on earth?) There is none, the poet answers. When Pears first received the rather terrifying score, he wrote Henze a not-so-cryptic postcard. 'Gibt es auf Erden ein Tenor . . . ?'

As I painfully drummed it into my skull (I'm a very slow learner and no master at reading pitch), it was quite clear to me that this is music that will endure to summon up new worlds and show us new horizons.

1999

In January 2010 I took part in the first performances of Hans Werner Henze's new work, commissioned by the Santa Cecilia Orchestra in Rome. Opfergang *is a setting of an extraordinary, eccentric, uncategorisable poem by Franz Werfel, the Viennese writer famed as one of Alma Mahler's husbands and the author of* The Song of Bernadette. *A fugitive, one of life's victims, an obvious Freudian subject, meets, at night, by the river bank of a city, a well-cared-for white dog. They engage in a mutually incomprehensible dialogue which ends with the protagonist abusing and finally strangling the animal and throwing him into the river. The fugitive, pursued by the police, escapes and transcends his troubles. The dog's ghost sings from the firmament. A work, then, that reflects Henze's love of animals – he has been a committed vegetarian for years, and a dog-owner too – but also an ability to confront the sadism and complexity embodied in human relationships. I sang the part of the dog – happily it was a concert performance – and I was reunited with John Tomlinson as Der Fremde, the stranger (I had first sung with him as a child in 1977 in a production of* Werther *at English National Opera). Tony Pappano conducted.*

The Tempest

Thomas Adès's first full-scale opera – with a libretto 'after Shakespeare' by Meredith Oakes – is about to have its premiere at the Royal Opera. And, intriguingly, this young composer has chosen one of Shakespeare's late plays, probably the last he wrote as a solo venture, and one whose epilogue – 'Now my charms are all o'erthrown, / what strength I have's my own' – has often been reimagined as the playwright's own theatrical valediction.

From a dramatic point of view, *The Tempest* seems to break all the rules. It looks, at first, a somewhat daunting choice for operatic adaptation. Formally a comedy (though categorised as a romance for more than a century, along with *The Winter's Tale*, *Pericles* and *Cymbeline*), it is probably the least conventionally plotted of any of Shakespeare's plays. It starts with the shipwrecking storm of the title, and most of the plot – concerning the feud that led to the magician Prospero's exile from Milan to the mysterious island where the action is set – has happened before the beginning of the play. We hear about it only in an exceptionally long speech Prospero makes to his daughter, Miranda. Motives are confused. Suspense is absent. Revelations are contrived. It's not obvious operatic material, except inasmuch as it starts with a storm (operatic storms are plentiful – in places such as Britten's Borough, Gershwin's Catfish Row and 'Verdi's Cyprus' to name but three). It does offer a handful of enticing set-pieces (the magical banquet offered to the shipwrecked, suddenly removed by a 'quaint device';

Prospero's account of his majestic occult powers; or Ferdinand and Miranda discovered playing chess); but the comic scenes are impenetrable and often fall flat on stage.

From another point of view, *The Tempest* cries out for music. 'The isle is full of noises, sounds and sweet airs,' Caliban, the island's indigenous man-monster, says. The play is full of lyrics, more than any of Shakespeare's works: 'Full fathom five', 'Where the bee sucks', 'Come unto these yellow sands'. But there are also Stephano's and Trinculo's comical drunken catches, and many musical stage directions ('solemn music', 'solemn and strange music', 'soft music', 'a strange, hollow and confused noise').

Two twentieth-century British composers in particular saw the opportunities the play presented – there are Michael Tippett's *Songs for Ariel*, and Benjamin Britten at one stage planned music for a John Gielgud film version. But in doing so, they were echoing the play's far longer history. Indeed, between the Restoration and the Victorian era, the original Shakespeare was almost submerged under music. William Davenant and John Dryden started the process, adding music and characters, while cutting out two-thirds of Shakespeare's text. Thomas Shadwell went further, with a mixed bag of a score by various composers (including Purcell) which some have – mistakenly, I think – called an opera. Increasingly, over a hundred and fifty years, the play became an entertainment, with music and machinery, an immensely popular quasi-vaudeville, a money-spinner rather than the Delphic utterance or post-colonial meditation modern audiences have come to expect.

An opera based on *The Tempest* would be something very different – not a patchwork or ragbag but something growing out of its central musical metaphor and the quintessentially Renaissance idea of music itself as a form of sympathetic magic. Shakespeare's island hums with music; but the play uses music for its own theatrical purposes. An opera would have to make a new *Tempest* out of musical materials that have their own logic. For, if opera is drama, as the musicologist Joseph Kerman famously had it, the drama has to be in the music.

This is the route Adès and Oakes have followed, ruthlessly reworking the plot and, perhaps most controversially, ditching the original text. In its place we have a rhyming and half-rhyming libretto – a fabulous aid to comprehensibility in the opera house – modern in diction, only very occasionally evoking the Shakespearean cadence. As a song singer, I can regret the loss of such words to relish in the voice; but for the creation of a music drama, five weeks of rehearsal have convinced me of its necessity. The plot has been significantly realigned. Themes of redemptive love, parental affection and reconciliation are worked out in the music in a very different way from in the play. It's textually less open-ended and ambiguous than Shakespeare – Adès points to the simplifications Arrigo Boito had to make for his libretto for Guiseppe Verdi's *Otello* – but music inevitably retains its own sort of open-endedness.

Ferdinand's and Miranda's love music is of a ravishing beauty. The reconciliation quintet of the third act, while verbally simple, is at the same time highly wrought musically (a brilliantly constructed passacaglia) and strikingly memorable. Prospero's great Act V speech, which Shakespeare drew directly from Ovid's evocation of Medea, becomes in the opera a moment of parallel metaphysical power, mighty music indeed (and I haven't even heard the orchestration yet). In general, the musical language of the opera makes a journey from the curdled accents of Act I, overshadowed by Prospero's rage and thirst for vengeance, to the simple, natural music of the island that emerges at the end. Prospero departs. Ariel and Caliban reclaim their inheritance.

I'm playing Caliban, so I may be biased, but Caliban is one of the reasons you would want to make an opera of *The Tempest* in the first place. He is, this 'deformed and salvage slave', as the First Folio decribes him, one of the great Shakespearean icons. He's funny, visionary, violent, childish and poignant by turns. The question of where our sympathy should lie in regard to Caliban has dominated critical discourse about the play for the past fifty years. The colonial interpretation, in which Caliban is a dispossessed aboriginal and Shakespeare an acute critic of Renaissance colonialism, is something the opera seems at first sight to sidestep. In a sense, however, it pushes it to the limit. Caliban's capacity for a sort of nobility is knitted into his music and underlined in the plot.

As a singer at what you might call the highbrow end of the business, engaged in art-song and accustomed to singing princes or fresh-faced juveniles in opera, I'm hardly central casting for the hairy wild man to which audiences have long been accustomed (though Adès's decision to write the role for me is something compared to the unlikely but successful casting of Simon Russell Beale as Ariel a few years back). In the opera, as in the play, there is something distinctly noble about Caliban. But his nobility here is more focused. My favourite line, Caliban as toddler – 'I must have my dinner', preceding one of his great anti-Prospero rants – has gone. So too have the blood-curdling details of his plans for Prospero's murder. Most significantly, perhaps,

Stephano and Trinculo are clearly Caliban's stooges in the plot against Prospero. A quibble about sovereignty in the original play – 'I am all the subjects that you have, which once was mine own king,' Caliban complains to Prospero, anticipating Defoe's *Robinson Crusoe* – has become a notion in the opera that Caliban was king before Prospero's arrival. He tells us so on his first appearance; and when Prospero leaves he remains on the island and resumes his proper dignity and crown. In the play, by contrast, he goes to Prospero's cell to make dinner, servile and resolved to be a better monster.

As a result, that beautiful Shakespearean speech of Caliban's about the music of the island, strangely buried in one of the tedious comical scenes, is dramatically liberated and transformed. It bisects the action, offering a vision of what the island could be like without Prospero's curdling rage. The aria that Adès has written for Caliban at that moment is one of those moments singers thank composers for, truly lyrical, deeply felt, sophisticated – not least rhythmically – and ultimately memorable.

This is a dangerous game, of course, just as dangerous as messing with England's national poet. Writing this sort of music is exposing, and something many twentieth-century composers avoided for fear of the easy accusation of sentimentality. The avoidance in art of what might be seen as sentimental is surely a phenomenon rooted in historical circumstance. Its roots were manifold: snobbery and the fear of mass culture that John Carey has eloquently described; the rejection of a parody Victorianism; and the trauma of war and genocide in the citadels of European culture.

A living opera tradition means leaving those ghosts behind. Janáček, Britten, Berg were all unafraid to take this risk. It's a high-wire act, maintaining a personal and contemporary idiom that can accommodate sentiment and legitimate melody. *The Tempest* inhabits a thoroughly organic sound-world, with a musical language that speaks of human feeling and stakes its credibility on moments of the most transparent beauty. For once, ambition and accessibility go hand in hand.

2004

I remember sitting next to Tom in the auditorium at Covent Garden as Ferdinand's and Miranda's love scene was rehearsed on stage. A cymbal sound at the climax of the music in the orchestra; a kiss on stage. 'Too much?' he queried, answering his own question with a definitive no.

Index

Index

Index

Index

Index

Index